A Child's Tapestry of War

To David,

A Child's Tapestry of War

Denmark
1940 - 1945

Enjoy the story from a different point of view

Anne Ipsen

Anne Ipsen

Beaver's Pond Press

J. Ipsen "Hvide mennesker og busser," from *Spejling af virkeligheden, Prosa Almanak* 1990, Gallo Forlaget, copyright 1990 by J. Ipsen. A translation by Anne and Johannes Ipsen is included as Chapter 11 with permission of J. Ipsen and the publisher.

Photographs are from the author's personal collection.
Cover design by Mori Studio.

ISBN: 1-890676-11-X

Printed in the United States of America.

J I H G F E D C B A

Beaver's Pond Press

5125 Danen's Drive
Edina, MN 55439-1465

To Mor and Far,
to other members of my family who were there,
and for those who were yet to come.

∾

My thanks to Carol and Jay for their enthusiasm and support;
the South Minneapolis Writer's Group for advice;
and for the encouragement of many friends.

PROLOGUE

A Country Occupied

The Second World War started in Europe when Great Britain and France declared war on Germany following Hitler's blitzkrieg invasion of Poland on the first of September, 1939. By the following spring the German army had defeated and occupied Denmark, Norway, and central Europe. In early June the British forces were pushed off the continent in the famous retreat from Dunkirk, and France was occupied as well. In southern Europe, Spain was fascist, Portugal in denial, Italy allied with Germany, and Greece and the Balkans overrun. Further north, only Sweden and Switzerland succeeded in remaining neutral throughout the war.

I was born in Denmark and lived in Copenhagen with my parents until just after the war. On the morning of April 9, 1940, we awoke to find that Denmark had been invaded by Germany. Their navy needed the ports on the west coast of Norway on the North Sea, and access from the German ports on the Baltic, around the eastern and northern coasts of Denmark. They also needed the food and manufactured products of Danish farming and ship building industries. The Norwegians, with the help of the British, attempted in vain to fight off the Germans. Denmark, however, had a non-aggression treaty with Hitler, and we confidently expected to remain neutral as we had during the First World War.

That April morning our *naïveté* was rudely shattered. At 5 a.m., the government received a note from Berlin claiming that Germany had 'evidence' of a plan to use Scandinavia as a battleground and an announcement that Hitler therefore was making Denmark and Norway 'protectorates.' Innocent-looking ferries and merchant vessels with German soldiers hidden below decks had already entered the Copenhagen harbor. At dawn they emerged and marched to the king's nearby palace. The sporadic fighting was nearly over by the time we awoke and discovered that king and government had surrendered. The last time Denmark had been at war, also hopelessly, was in 1864 when Germany, lead by Bismarck, had invaded our unprepared, indefensible and peaceful country and occupied the southern part of the peninsula of Jylland until 1920. This bitter lesson of military ambition, now had to be learned again.

At first the king and government went along with the useful fiction that Denmark was being 'protected' by Germany and that we were not at war. This allowed life to remain nearly normal and the government to remain in power—for a while. The true state of affairs was a little harder to explain to the rest of the world. However, as we found out later, the Danish ambassador to the United States was very persuasive and managed to convince Roosevelt that Denmark would *never* side with Germany. Denmark became the unknown ally.

The Danish people also tried to ignore the violation of accustomed freedom. Gradually frustration overcame lethargy; the covert resistance movement became more and more active; and people became more and more uncooperative through spontaneous acts of nuisance known as 'passive resistance.' The Underground began as isolated cells, supplied by airdrops of explosives from England. Gradually a well-organized underground government evolved, spurred by a series of intolerable events; Parliament resigned in protest, leaving the country to be administered by the civil service; and a remarkable general strike moved an unacceptably early curfew to later in the evening. On orders from Hitler, the Germans finally attempted to send Danish Jews to concentration camps, but the people, and especially the police, were remarkably successful in helping most of them escape. Sabotage of factories and railroads by the Resistance continued to escalate and seriously hampered shipment of food and machinery to Germany.

Denmark was reasonably self-sufficient in food because of an efficient, well-organized, and experienced agriculture but the country had few natural resources except for the ingenuity of the people. The lack of imported raw materials and the draining food shipments to Germany imposed more and more scarcities and rationing. However, while the last years of the war were grim, the hardships were mild compared to the horrors that were taking place in the surrounding countries. We changed our habits of eating but never went to bed hungry, were sometimes chilly but never truly cold, afraid but seldom in real danger. A thousand Danes were executed or died in camps, but none of our fathers nor brothers left home to be killed at a distant front. The worst of times was nothing compared to the tales we heard of bombings in England, starvation in Norway, and devastation of families everywhere.

Those five years of The War, as we always called it, were a strange time for me to learn the necessary lessons of preadolescence, a very different time. They included that part of my childhood which psychologists call the 'latency' period, a time before adolescence when development appears dormant, but much of the later character is fixed. That surprisingly protected and happy childhood in the midst of a very abnormal world did much to mold my character. Denmark also was in latency as the overt battles of war swirled around us while the inner turmoil and growing resistance gradually eroded life as it should have been and threatened to erupt into full rebellion. My awareness of the peculiarities of this existence grew as the rest of the country gradually arose to fight the unacceptable. In the beginning, my egocentric concerns were that of any little girl. Five years of maturing increased my understanding, but so did the pressures of occupation and war.

In telling these stories of a little girl's strange life, I have tried to remain faithful to the spirit of my memories as seen through the eyes of a young child and yet to accurately reflect the historical events. I have taken obvious liberties in reconstructing conversations, and added color and dimension to those black-and-white pictures with adult interpretations. My memories are vivid images like those of a medieval tapestry, woven from the fine threads of everyday life. They are filled with the colorful mille fleurs from a happy childhood and a white unicorn of fantasy encircled by family, but with an ominous backdrop of hunters in green—German soldiers.

ONE

Mørkelækningsrullegardiner

The beginning of my consistent childhood memories coincides with the German occupation of Denmark during the Second World War. It was the morning of April 9, 1940, four days before my birthday. My parents and I were standing by the living room window of our apartment in Copenhagen, looking up at the German planes flying overhead.

"They must be going to Norway," Mor said. Like all Danish children, I called my parents Mor and Far, short for the formal Moder and Fader.

Mor knew that our Norwegian neighbors to the north were fighting the Germans in air and sea battles. However, 'war' and even 'Norway' meant nothing to me; after all, I was not yet five.

"I'll go get a newspaper and find out what's going on," said Far, buckling the leather belt around his waist and across the front of his army uniform. He was a doctor, completing his compulsory military service in the reserves of the Medical Corps. The leather belt was a relic from a more innocent time when army officers carried swords.

Soon he returned, bounding up the stairs to our third floor apartment, as usual taking the steps two at a time instead of waiting for the lumbering elevator.

"And then the newsboy said, 'Hey Pops, you better get out of that uniform—we've been invaded!'" Far told us breathlessly.

"I suppose I should report to the Army Hospital for orders," he said doubtfully. "But maybe I should take off my uniform first," he added with an ironic smile, unbuckling his belt. What is a soldier supposed to do when his country has been invaded and nobody told him?

By the end of the day, he was dismissed from further service and could concentrate on his regular job at the State Serum Institute where he worked in the department responsible to the League of Nations for the standardization of vaccines. The army uniform was hung in the back of the closet.

My parents always played honeymoon bridge after dinner and talked about the events of the day. Usually they talked about boring everyday events with Far relating the happenings of his day and Mor prompting, "And what did you say then?" Now it became more exciting, though most of the details and politics went over my head. I stayed to listen hoping that Mor wouldn't chase me off to my room to play. Both of my parents were marvelous storytellers and tried to explain the mysteries of this new world to me. Mor excelled at relating her everyday adventures and describing the people she met, past and present. Far knew everything from literature and history to science and music. He could make anything interesting with his dry sense of humor and ready smile.

"That morning the king saw his wonderful guards slaughtered and stopped the fighting. You know, they pick the best soldiers to guard the palace and only the ones who are tall enough. They have to be as tall as the king," Far said, shuffling the cards.

I imagined the tall king standing on the balcony of the palace and looking down at his guards in their tall fuzzy hats lying wounded on the parade ground.

Christian X had always been a symbol of rectitude and dignity, riding through the city on his horse every morning, so punctual that people bragged they could set their watches by his passing. He now became a focal point of national pride and the hero of wondrous tales of stubborn passive resistance. Every morning he continued to ride, alone and unguarded as always, maintaining an appearance of normalcy. Mor showed me his picture in the paper—a tall soldier on a horse, sporting a dapper mustache and smiling paternally down at his people. His uniform looked just like the one Far never wore again, but hid in the back of the coat closet, just in case.

"They're still fighting at the border, down near Sønderborg where your grandfather lives. Everybody expected they would invade there, as Bismarck did in 1864," Far explained.

"Hitler says he is protecting us from the British! How can he expect us to believe that?" Mor complained. The king and the government went along with this useful fiction which allowed life to remain nearly normal and the government to remain in power—for a while.

A few days after that memorable morning, I looked down at the long rolls of black paper lying on the hall floor. "What's that?"

"Mørkelægningsrullegardiner."

"Huh?"

"Mørke-lægnings-rulle-gardiner."

I tried to say the strange difficult word for blackout curtains, as long as the black rolls of paper waiting on the floor to be installed.

The word parts are glued together and literally mean 'darkness-laying-roller-shades.'

"The Germans are making us cover the windows at night so the English war planes can't use the city lights to find their way," Mor explained. I couldn't believe they really worked. Light leaked out at the sides and I could see the outline of our windows when we were outside after dark. Wouldn't the pilots see us just as well from the air? And why would the English want to bomb us when we were on their side?

Oh, how we hated those curtains; they became a metaphor for those five years: laying a darkness on life and land. Closing them at dusk became an evening ritual, a reminder of what was out there but always opened at bedtime so we could see the twinkling stars shining from a free world beyond war.

Mor at a lunch stop in Southern Europe, probably summer 1938 or '39.

I remember the previous summer when I visited my godfather's country house, Myretuen —'The Anthill'. The large, rambling summerhouse by the beach was always filled with people: relatives, seamstresses, friends, servants on holiday, etc. I always thought of these visitors as 'the ants' as they swarmed around the dinner table or walked in a long line down to the beach to swim. The family had more or less adopted my mother when as a young woman she moved to Copenhagen and became friends with a daughter of the house. There was a grandchild, a few years older than I, and we were occasional playmates. That summer I stayed there while my parents attended their usual, but as it turned out, last scientific summer meeting somewhere in southern Europe.

Mor kept an album of postcards and photographs from these summer trips that I loved to look at, imagining myself in these exciting places. Three loose cards were addressed to me at Myretuen with pictures of Susak (in Yugoslavia, I think), Padua and Florence—ordinary little greetings, dated late in August 1939.

Mor and Far were expected back from their trip but they were very late. They had called the night before, and I was allowed to stand on a stool and say hello on the old-fashioned telephone in the hallway. I could barely hear anything through the funny thing held to my ear and had to push a button by the mouthpiece on the wall and shout when I wanted to say something. Now I waited and waited on the driveway in my best dress, homesick and very tired of having to use my guest manners. There was no sign of our little Opel on the sandy road.

Then suddenly they were there. "Is that beautiful lady with the pointy chin really Mor?" I thought to myself and was amazed that her familiar face looked so different.

The grownups were full of excited talk of adventures and politics. My parents had been delayed driving north through central Europe.

The invasion of Czechoslovakia and the defeat of Poland followed that September with the declaration of war. What did I understand or care about all that; my parents were back and we could go home.

Now, only seven months later, there were to be no more summer trips for my parents, no more scientific meetings, no more of my staying home while they went to exotic places. When Danish children play 'house' it's called Far-Mor-Børn, which literally means 'Father-Mother-Children.' That's what we did now. The strange goings on around us drew our little family closer together, Far-Mor-Anne. There wasn't much else to do, with no car, less of everything, none of some. Of course, to me life seemed precisely as it was supposed to be, filled with family, friends, trips to the cabin, school. Eventually some of the external world filtered in as I overheard the grownups talk and tell stories and began to understand that all was not as it should be. Life changed dramatically from what it had been, but only gradually did I come to realize the difference between freedom and occupation, peace and war.

We had lived in our apartment in Christianshavn only about a year. Before that I dimly remember living in an old building on a dark street with a church at the end of it, also in Christianshavn. This district of Copenhagen is on a large island called Amager, separated by a narrow channel of water from the main city. Amager hangs like a large impudent tongue off Copenhagen harbor, then connected to the old capital by two drawbridges. Copenhagen is also on an island, called Sjælland, 'Zealand' on English speaking maps. It is the biggest island in this country consisting of hundreds of islands and one large peninsula, Jylland.

In an early memory, I was down on the narrow little street playing with a ball. "How old are you, little girl?" asked a friendly woman.

"Three and three-knarters," was my proud and precise answer.

I was four when we moved from that apartment to the place where we lived when the war started. That new red brick and very modern building was on Stormøllevej—'Big Mill Road' further out on the island. I always wanted to go to the end of the street and see the mill. Was it still there, right at the edge of the city? That is the street where I finally mastered the jump rope. As I ran up and down the sidewalk, the rope slapped on the cement in front of me and tangled in my feet. Over and over I practiced, until one day something clicked and the rope went around and around smoothly, making a satisfying rhythmic thump on the pavement as it slid under my feet.

That was also where one of the big boys, barely adolescent, made a strange suggestion, "Come into the entry and let me see you."

"Huh?"

"Pull down your pants, I want to see what a girl looks like."

"Can't you ask your mor? Or do you have a sister?" I suggested helpfully. He looked shocked.

I felt sorry for him, but there was a limit! "His mor really should show him," I thought. I knew what boys looked like because at the cabin we often went swimming or sunbathed unencumbered. I thought everyone lived like that, open and free.

There was a playground on the roof of the building, fenced and with netting all around the top so the resident children could play ball. For some reason we didn't go up there often; the street was more interesting.

That morning of April 9 was only three days before my fifth birthday. My presents had already been bought, including a wonderful blue shiny scooter, made in America and called a 'Johnny-wheel.' It was very special. The most unusual part was a lever-pedal on the base. By

11

standing on this pedal with one foot in front of the other, much as on a skate board but pumping up and down, I could make the Johnny-wheel go very fast. There was room for a friend to sit folded up on the pedal while I squeezed one foot behind her and pushed with the other. It quickly became a favorite toy, the vehicle for many imaginary travels in the play yard and handy transportation for trips in the neighborhood.

Far and I were returning home one Sunday afternoon from his lab at the Serum Institute where he worked. Mor had very advanced ideas about the importance of shared parenting, so Far often took me along to the lab while he checked the mice in their round glass cages. I was scooting ahead when I skidded on some gravel and tumbled over the handlebars. Screams and tears. Far ran, fearing that the injury was as bad as the screams were loud. "Does he really love me that much, to run so fast for a skinned knee?" I thought, my self-conscious watching. I always had this second part of me, separate from my physical self; a critic riding on my shoulder that saw and remembered.

My parents had decided I was too young to get a bike for my birthday and had bought the Johnny-wheel instead. Two months later I got the bike anyway: a shiny black one with big blocks on the pedals so my short legs could reach. We sold the car to the Serum Institute because we could no longer buy gas. We didn't use it in the city anyway, and there were not going to be summer trips to Italy and Yugoslavia for a while. The biggest problem was how to get us to the cabin, some thirty miles north of town and nine miles from the nearest train station. The new bike was practical transportation; it was not a toy like the Johnny-wheel, but a necessity.

I practiced balancing and pedaling along Stormøllevej with Far running behind and holding the back of the seat. "She didn't need me to hold on for very long!" he later bragged to Mor.

My new bicycle, on the road in back of cabin in Esrum, north of Copenhagen.

She had watched the drama from our balcony and agreed with him, "It's all that practice on the Johnny-wheel."

By the time the war was over, five years later, the bike was not so shiny, the blocks had long since been taken off the pedals, and the seat was pushed up as far as it would go. My legs had grown too long, but we made do. We could not buy a new bigger bike. Even a flat tire was a major problem, for new tires were scarce, imported rubber not to be had, and ersatz rubber undependable.

A few months later Mor said, "We're moving again! We gave up our lease because we were supposed to go for a long visit to America. Now with the war we can't go."

The America visit was news to me, but I soon forgot about that. I puzzled over what a lease was as I packed my toys in a box Mor put on the floor of my room. I was drinking a glass of milk and put it down next to me, accidentally knocking it over. In a desperate

13

attempt to hide my carelessness, I ran to the kitchen and brought back a dishrag. After mopping up the spilt milk, I squeezed it into the glass intending to drink the evidence. It looked terrible and smelled worse and I surreptitiously poured the mess into the toilet. Then the moving men came and carried our lives to our new apartment.

TWO

By The Rampart

The new apartment building—an architectural marvel that was barely finished—was a redevelopment in the middle of an ancient slum. It also is in Christianshavn but closer to downtown than our old place, just inside the fortifications that circled Copenhagen in older times. The high hill of the rampart has long since been made into a large park with a convenient sledding hill on one side, wonderful trees to climb at the top, and graceful paths down to the water on the other side. The water was the wide deep moat, but is now a crescent-shaped lake, perfect for ice-skating in the coldest part of winter. Market Street crosses the water on a bridge and cuts through the grassy mound of the rampart. There used to be gates here, closed at night, one of the entrances to the fortified city. The old yellow brick guardhouse is still there, a silent anachronistic observer of the modern traffic whizzing by. During the war it was also mute, perhaps in shame that it had not served its intended purpose of keeping the residents of the city safe. The enemy had snuck in while the guards of the country slept.

The address of our new home was exotic: *Ved Volden*— 'By The Rampart'. The apartment building is a complex of three wings, surrounding a large shallow pool. The fourth side is open to the grassy mound of the rampart park. The city planners made the architect leave a gap between two of the wings so *Vor Frelsers Kirke*— 'the Church of Our Savior' could be seen from the park. I think the church was built in the seventeenth century by the imaginative architect-king, Christian IV for whom Christianshavn is named, but I may be wrong. This king built most of the other buildings with copper-covered spires that give Copenhagen its distinctive skyline, so the assumption is natural. The tower has a fantastic, verdigris green, tall

By The Rampart and the Church of Our Savior.
Our apartment was in the wing to the right of
the picture.

spire with a helical walkway on the outside, all the way up to a gold ball with a gold statue on top. It was an occasional treat to go up that spiral, looking down at the city below and the golden ball above. Bells in the tower marked the quarter hour, tolled on the hour, and played hymns four times during the day. The nine o'clock hymn was my evensong and nightly lullaby.

The shallow, decorative wading pond filled most of the center of the courtyard of the apartment complex and was surrounded on three sides by a generous border of prickly barberry bushes separating the pond from a wide asphalt drive and parking lot. Two huge weeping willows stood on either side, their trailing branches hanging so low that all of the children in the yard could hide under them. On the left were two metal animal sculptures, spewing arcs of water over the pond. One sculpture was of a walrus with a hollow body that looked like it had started life as a sailing buoy. It had an opening at the bottom and was so fat that five of us children could squeeze inside for a secret but cramped meeting house.

The drive around the pond was empty of cars because of the war. It was perfect for ball games, bikes, hopscotch, jumping rope, roller skates—and the Johnny-wheel! There were always kids to play with, of all ages. The best times were when we joined together for large group games of cops and robbers, or tag, or to build snow forts for snowball fights—that is, if the big boys could be persuaded to stop teasing and join us. We invented intricate games that could only be played with a large gang. Right below the balcony of our apartment, in a wide sunny part of the drive, there was a very large sandbox with a concrete railing to keep toddlers from climbing out. I spent many happy hours there with the other children, building sand castles and marble runs. What a fantastic playground.

On the rampart side of the pond there was a low fence with a beech hedge shutting out non-residents. Along the hedge was a long continuous bench where mothers sat to enjoy the view of the fountains in the pond, the church spire in the break between the wings of the apartment complex, and the children at play. The pond was only a couple of feet deep, ideal for wading, sailing model boats, and winter skating.

By the next summer, the fountains were turned off to conserve electricity. During the last year of the war, the water was drained to provide an open storage area for coal and wood for the furnace. Our enterprising apartment manager had scrounged this supply from some unknown source and thus managed to keep us warm during the final cold winter. The huge mound of coal was ugly, and the piles of wooden logs became rat infested. We children adapted quickly, inventing new games and building caves in the log piles. We thought of the manager as the mean-man-who-is-always-chasing-us-away-from-the-best-places-to-play. The grownups thought him unusually resourceful under trying circumstances, taking care of us all with imagination and forethought.

Our new apartment was smaller than the one on Stormøllevej, but we needed to find a place to live in a hurry and it was new and modern. There was a sunny living room with a large balcony overlooking the center courtyard and pond. Next to that was the dining room which my parents used as their bedroom; and off a little back hall were the kitchen, bathroom, and my small room. The kitchen had a built-in refrigerator, and the bathroom had heated pipes under the floor to keep our feet warm in the winter. Much good these modern marvels did us when shortly thereafter the hot water was turned off and the electricity and gas rationed. In the communal basement was a shared laundry room with large drying ovens and big heated washtubs for boiling linens. There was also a commercial laundry where Mor took our sheets and Far's shirts.

We started to have air raids at night. The siren sounded whenever British, and later American planes were sighted, heading for the Sound, the narrow strip of water between Denmark and Sweden, to lay mines or make bombing trips to eastern Germany. Jokingly we complained that they woke us up twice with the sirens: when the planes were on the way out and on their way back.

The residents of the apartment building were told to go to special rooms in the basement where all the windows were blocked on the outside by big wooden boxes filled with sand. The greatest danger was from stray anti-aircraft shells since there was little point in bombing Denmark itself, so after a while, when the siren sounded we just moved away from the windows and stopped going to the basement. Besides, I was such a sound sleeper that it was impossible to wake me up enough to get me down the stairs.

I only remember two bombings of Copenhagen during the whole five years: one at the beginning and one at the end. The first one happened soon after we moved into Ved Volden. Far was home early from the lab to look after me while Mor went downtown on some errands. The sirens went off late in the afternoon.

"Let's go to the window and see all the people run for the shelters!" said Far, trying to reassure me that there was no danger. He had long since stopped worrying about bombings. We stood together looking out the bedroom window. People were running across the playground. Two planes flew low over the rooftops of houses in the near distance.

Just as Far said, "Look at those German planes hurry for cover," we saw a column of black smoke reaching from the ground toward the planes. Then there was a loud explosion. Far grabbed my hand and we ran for the basement, but the bombing was over.

"Imagine, he was in such a hurry, he made me put on my summer coat and it doesn't even fit anymore," I later told Mor with great relish.

"Fathers don't understand such practical things as the difference between summer and winter coats," Mor joked.

She had come home hours later with exciting tales. She had been on the streetcar on her way home and had just reached the bridge to Christianshavn when the siren went off. "They told us all to go to the shelter under the bridge. We were going down the stairs just as the bombs fell on the other side of the water. There was an unexploded bomb on the bridge so they wouldn't let us go home for ages."

The planes we had seen were English, not German. They were aiming at the Burmeister and Wain ship builders, located by the channel between Copenhagen and Amager Island, forced to build submarine engines for the German navy. Unfortunately, the only bomb to fall even near the target never exploded. The very black smoke we had seen from the window came from the sugar factory next to the inner harbor. Other bombs fell on the bridge and damaged the church at the end of the street where I played when I was "three and three-knarters." Why wasn't I scared? I only remember the excitement and thinking that Mor always had all the fun and told great stories!

The Resistance, called the Underground, was just getting organized. After the bombing fiasco, they contacted England and suggested that if anything needed blowing up, they should air-drop the necessary supplies. The Underground would make sure the right buildings were destroyed. We couldn't spare any more sugar factories or churches!

The stories of the exploits of the Underground were passed by word of mouth during the rest of the war. Far would entertain Mor and me at dinner with exciting tales of heroes and tricks played on the "stupid Germans." These stories were better than the adventures of Robin Hood.

We had a daily routine, Mor and I. First came housework: I made my bed while Mor did the dishes. On the day laundry was picked up, we took off the white pillowcases and sheets and stuffed them into one of the pink striped covers for the down quilts. Next Far's shirts were counted and added to the load. One time we brought the bundle to the big laundry ourselves. Peering over the counter, I could barely see through the steam to where several uniformed girls with little caps on their hair were feeding damp linens through large rollers. The linens were not 'ironed' but 'mangled' on huge machines that pressed them between heated rollers as wide as a sheet.

There was a little back balcony off our kitchen with a garbage shoot behind a little round porthole door. I was helping Mor by emptying the waste basket. "No mo-o-ore—," a haunting voice echoed up the shoot.

"Mor, Mor, the garbage shoot spoke to me. It really did!"

Milk, bread and rolls, still warm from the oven, were delivered every morning very early, but we shopped every day for other supplies because our wonderful built-in refrigerator, which seemed quite roomy, soon had to be turned off to save electricity. Mor took money out of a little envelope kept in the desk and showed me how she divided the household money into four envelopes, one for each week of the month. "When we were first married and had very little money, I set up this system," she explained. "I figured out that it was hard if we ran out of money the last four days of the month, but we could easily manage for one day if we ran out at the end of the week."

"I'm no good with money," Mor complained. She always had doubts about her own abilities but had unbounded confidence in mine. I was continually impressed with her common sense and was never convinced by her self-doubts that were so manifestly untrue.

There were no supermarkets so we went to a different little store for each kind of food or other supplies. We walked along Market

Street and down the steps to the little basement hardware store called Brugsen. Brug means 'use' and it certainly was full of useful things: broom handles for playing hopscotch, fluffy soap flakes for laundry and dishwashing, and vinegar for rinsing my hair when Mor shampooed it in the kitchen sink. We went to the pharmacy to get Bayer aspirin, Colgate toothpaste, and black licorice syrup for my cough. I was addicted to the cough syrup, the pharmacist's wonderful concoction that was worth getting a cold for, but soon the supply of licorice root dried up with the rest of the imports.

The fruit and vegetable store was across the street and down a little alley by the market square. Boxes spilled out onto the narrow sidewalk and were filled with apples and pears, potatoes and onions, carrots and cabbages, but no imported oranges and bananas. Tropical fruits were a dream from before.

We had to go to the meat market to get cold cuts and salads for sandwiches. Far brought his lunch to work every day. He had a long thin aluminum container, just the right size for two slices of Danish pumpernickel to fit side by side and just thick enough to stack them and their generous toppings two deep. Each square slice, called a 'round' of bread, was cut in half and 'scraped' with a thin layer of rationed butter. Then cold cuts, liver paté, herring, salads, sliced leftover potatoes, hard-boiled eggs, tomatoes, or cheese were piled on top and decorated with chopped greens or other garnishes. A little rectangle of parchment paper, made just to fit a half-slice, was put on top to separate the layers. This was the classic Danish lunch of open-faced sandwiches.

When my parents were first married, Far came home for lunch every day. At first, Mor made a big platter of sandwiches for the two of them, but complained, "Before I could finish even one, Far had eaten all the rest."

"Well, with six kids at home, I learned to eat fast or there were no seconds," Far would explain.

"I started to divide the sandwiches onto two plates but that didn't work either," Mor added. "Finally I told him that I had married him for better or for worse, but not for lunch. So now he eats at work."

Several times a week we took the streetcar across the bridge to the fish market on the other side of the narrow channel that divides Christianshavn from the main part of Copenhagen. The live fish swam in big tanks awaiting their death sentences as we made our choices. "I'll have a smoked mackerel for lunch tomorrow, and please fillet those two flounders for tonight," said Mor, pointing to the left corner of the tank. We watched the man scoop up the flounders with a big net and deftly filleted the meat off the bones with a thin knife. Mor turned to me and added, "We'll get some parsley for your favorite sauce. You can chop it for me."

When we got home from shopping, Mor put the fillets in a bowl of water on the kitchen counter so they would stay moist for dinner. As Far walked in the door, we heard a soft noise and went to investigate. "Look, the fillets are so fresh they splashed water all over the counter. Muscles will keep contracting even after an animal is dead," explained Far. Doctors know all kinds of wonderful things like that.

Sometimes we went further downtown to the fancy meat market. I didn't like it there because the store was usually packed and I had to wait forever, squeezed between jabbering women who were clamoring for attention and larger cuts of meat. Mor talked with the clerk as if they were old friends while I impatiently tugged at her arm to go home. "I have to be friendly so she'll give me some meat," Mor said.

Meat was never really rationed because that required accounting for how much there was. If the Germans knew that Denmark actually had meat, they would have shipped most of it back to Germany or to the front. Thus, we pretended that there was very little, but a steady customer would be handed a wrapped package, take-it-or-leave-it. Sometimes it was frankfurters, sometimes a large roast. Smart shopper that Mor was, she was a 'steady customer' at several shops and gladly accepted whatever she could get. She developed her own novel recipes to take advantage of whatever we had.

Finally we rode home on the streetcar, Mor chatting with perfect strangers, ever the sympathetic listener.

"Can we go to Irma's?" I pleaded. This was one of a chain of small butter and cheese stores near our apartment, the forerunners of a large post-war chain of supermarkets. I loved to go there. During the early months of the war, a large variety of cheeses was displayed in the window. I was fascinated because water cascaded down on the inside of the glass to keep the humidity high and the cheese fresh. Later the window-waterfall was stopped to conserve electricity, the cheese and butter rationed, and the display no longer so lavish.

Inside the store, the butter was kept in large open barrels on a high shelf in back of the counter. "A pound of butter, please," Mor said. Nowadays, she would have asked for a half-kilo or 500 grams, but 'pound' was still in use then.

I watched in anticipation as the clerk placed a square of paper on the scale, turned to the shelf in back of her, and with a small wooden paddle extracted a mound of butter from the barrel above her head. She checked the weight on the scale and added a little more. Deftly she patted and pounded with the paddle to shape the yellow mound and, slipping her left hand under the piece of paper, squared the sides. She folded the paper over the top, creased the ends, and tucked them underneath. "*Værsgo*— here you are," (literally: 'be so good') she said as she handed me the neat little package in exchange for money and butter ration coupons. Other stores sold butter in little pre-wrapped blocks with pictures of Viking trumpets on them, but I liked watching the woman at Irma's better. I practiced patting and shaping little blocks of sand in the sandbox, pretending I was a shopkeeper.

"Stay out here," Mor said when we reached our final shop. "I need to change our order for delivery of bread and rolls, and I don't want them to see that I bought butter at Irma's." The strategies developed by the skilled war-time housewife were endless and very confusing.

It was time to think about school. The neighborhood was mostly poor, the apartment complex an oasis in a slum district and the local public school a rough place. I started kindergarten. I barely remember, partly because I didn't stay more than a few weeks, having promptly caught several colds. Anyway, I was young, shy, and happier at home.

Then came Christmas, and my favorite present was a spelling toy. The wooden letters moved in a ring around the edge of a tray and could be slid into a middle track to form words. I was fascinated. "She's teaching herself to read, we'd better hurry and get her into real school or she's going to be bored," Mor decided. Mor made all the decisions about the family. Far, the busy and absent-minded scientist, seemed content to leave the running of our lives to her, although every plan was thoroughly discussed during the after-dinner bridge game. We all knew that Far's wishes and opinions were consulted. I was not expected to have an opinion.

There was a small, private girl's school just two blocks away, *Døttre Skolen*— 'The Daughters' School.' What a stuffy, Victorian name. We went for an interview with the principal. I sat in her office, swallowed up by a large leather chair, to be inspected by the formidable old lady. Somehow Mor persuaded her that I was ready for first grade.

The normal starting age for first grade in Denmark is seven. Bishop Gruntvig, a nineteenth century reform educator, decreed that this was the age when children were ready for school. I think most children of that earlier era were taught at home by reading the Bible and first grade was merely the beginning of formal instruction. When I was a child, reading was to be taught by the experts at school, but seven was still the magic age. An exception was made and I started school a year early, just before my sixth birthday. For some reason, the year began April 1 at The Daughters' School. That was probably a tradition from its founding days a hundred years earlier when the more common August start had not yet become standard.

The photo album has an under-lit picture of my small classroom with about ten students, round-eyed at the big day. In another snapshot, I am standing in front of the building, my hair half out of my

On my way to school, a knapsack on my back, but no sword at my side. The boxes in the background are filled with sand to put out the fires caused by bombing.

hood. My arm is linked with a classmate's and we are giggling. I am wearing a school knapsack, not too different from the one on the soldier's back in my book of Hans Christian Andersen's *Fairy Tales*; the story of *The Tinder-box* that starts, "Left, right! Left, right! The soldier came marching down the road. Left, right! Left, right! He had his knapsack on his back and a sword at his side."

I had picked out my school bag in the leather goods store that had just opened around the corner. It was in the wing of the apartment complex, facing Market Street, right next to the candy store. The knapsack was a rigid box with leather shoulder straps and was covered in real sealskin. It was very grand.

For the first few days, Mor walked me the short distance to school, but soon I was allowed to go by myself. I had to cross busy Princess Street where the No. 8 streetcar started and walk by the Church of Our Savior. I was told to look both ways and wait for a break in the traffic. The first day on my own, Mor anxiously watched from the back balcony and I waved to her. As I stood there waiting for the traffic to clear, I wondered how her being way up there was going to keep me safe.

"I needn't have worried," she reported to Far that evening. "She stood on the curb for such a long time, waiting until there was no traffic at all. I thought she'd never get across."

The homeroom teacher taught us reading, writing (in Danish, of course), and social studies consisting of prehistoric legends. She advanced with us each year, so she remained my main teacher for the three and a half years I stayed at The Daughters' School. I suppose that system was designed to give elementary students a sense of stability and the teachers variety as they taught at different levels each year. On the other hand, if one were unlucky enough to draw a mean teacher, it could have been terrible. I was lucky. I remember little of the teacher except that she was very nice.

I was in bed with a spring cold, bored. "Read me a story," I begged.

"Read it yourself," said Far. The world's greatest dramatic reader of stories was busy with something else.

"The Princess and the Pea." I read out loud as we always did in school, haltingly at first, then gaining confidence. "The water ran down her hair, and in at the tip of her shoes and out again at the heels; and yet she claimed she was a real Princess."

"—and there it still is, unless a collector has taken it." My voice was hoarse from reading for such a long time as I triumphantly reached the end of the familiar tale on the second page. I could really read. That stuff we do in school really works!

I have always loved that story. Not only was it the first I read by myself, but it was so deliciously silly. Imagine judging the value of a princess, or any other girl, by how delicate she was. I can now admire the skill with which Hans Christian Andersen pulls the reader out onto the limb of an hyperbole. It is satire to nourish the budding feminist, and is not just for children.

Every morning the whole school met in the gymnasium for 'morning song' of hymns, The Lord's Prayer, and announcements. We marched in a double line, holding hands, the first grade in front. If anyone had a birthday, she was called to the podium and allowed to choose the hymns. In front of the whole school! This was supposed to be a treat? "I hope my birthday falls on a Sunday, or I'm sick, or nobody knows," I thought. A birthday tradition that I did like was to have a Danish flag on my desk for the day.

The hymnals were thick little books with tissue-thin pages edged in gold. The paper had to be thin because there were so many hymns, many written by the prolific Bishop Gruntvig himself and other gifted nineteenth century Danish poets. The tactile sensation of leafing through those translucent pages remains with me still; I can almost smell the gold.

I loved the singing as long as I could bury my shaky voice in the large assembly. At home we often sang songs while Far played the guitar. Mor liked to listen but never joined in because she couldn't carry a tune. "I never learned to sing, because my voice is so deep," she explained with a *non sequitur* that I never understood.

I felt good about my singing, until one year in school when the music teacher unwittingly but tactlessly made me self-conscious. At the beginning of the year she called each of us to the front of the class for a solo of our choice so she could hear our individual voices. I sang my little piece but was floored when the teacher condescendingly said, "That was much better than last year."

"Last year must have been terrible; I probably can't sing at all," I moaned to myself. "My voice is like Mor's, and I'll never be able to sing like Far."

We had a math teacher who also taught us how to embroider, knit, and crochet. I hated her. In first grade we embroidered a border on our sewing bags. The whole bag was made out of aida cloth. Since this fabric has large holes and a firm weave, it is easier for a beginning stitcher to use. I struggled with my stem, chain, and cross stitches and have hated aida cloth ever since. Stem stitches were called *kontor* a word that means 'office.' I constantly sought for logical explanations and reasoned that the stitches were so named because they had to be very precise, like office work, or they would look terrible, like mine.

The only office I knew was at Far's lab and that was very scientific. Actually, the correct word is from the French *contour* and describes the way these stitches can fit around a curved shape.

We also were supposed to learn to knit by making washcloths out of white cotton yarn. Mor had already taught me how to knit, so I started with confidence but soon lagged sadly behind the rest of my classmates. I dropped stitches and ripped out rows as my little rectangle became grubbier and grubbier. After each row, I hopefully folded one corner against the opposite to see if the miserable rag was square. Not yet. Why was I so hopelessly slow? I was many years an adult before the simple explanation dawned on me. At six, I might have been ready to learn to read, but my fine motor coordination was a year behind my seven-year-old classmates. It was so obvious, yet I don't think anyone realized the reason for my difficulty.

This formidable woman was not much better at teaching math. The accepted curriculum stressed mental arithmetic, never my forte. She would call on one of us to do the next problem in our head. When my turn came, my brain invariably froze and refused to do the simplest calculation. If she seemed to be following a pattern as she went around the room, I counted ahead in the book to find the problem that would be mine so I could have more time to figure out the answer. In later grades, I had trouble remembering the multiplication tables. One day we were doing written problems at our desks and I was stumped by 6 times 7. In desperation I lifted the top of my desk and peeked at the table printed in back of the book. The teacher saw me. "Anne, what *are* you doing?" she raged. "I won't tolerate cheating." I was so miserable that I resolved never to cheat again. It wasn't worth it.

One night I was doing my homework at the dining room table. Far looked over my shoulder and recoiled in horror when he saw my illegible numbers cramped in one corner of the page of the little bound exercise book. The next day my usually even-tempered father, who normally left all decisions on my upbringing and other household matters to Mor, stormed over to school. He stuck my notebook under the teacher's nose and demanded, "How can you expect her to learn mathematics when you can't even teach her to write the numbers underneath each other?"

"Well, you have to understand that Anne will never be able to learn mathematics," sputtered the surprised teacher. "As for the way she writes the numbers, are you having financial difficulties at home? She seems to be trying to save paper by writing way up in one corner of the page."

Far was thoroughly disgusted with this bungling idiot, but fortunately he dismissed her dire predictions of my future. He merely made sure that we practiced multiplication tables at breakfast. Mor was equally practical and concluded, "Well, if she can't do math, I had better make sure she learns to cook, has music lessons, and plenty of good books to read."

In later years, "Anne's inability to do math" became a family joke as I went on to major in mathematics at Radcliffe and eventually to receive my Ph.D. in statistics at Harvard. However, I was in graduate school before I stopped being ashamed of needing to write down my 'carries' and 'borrows' when adding or subtracting numbers.

Recess for the older grades was in the little enclosed school yard, crowded with yelling girls playing jump rope, hopscotch, and ball. To alleviate the crowding and keep the youngest students safe, the kindergarten and first grade students were allowed to play in cemetery of the Church of Our Savior, located next door. We crossed the street in two precise rows, compulsively put our feet along the lines formed by the cobblestones, and walked sedately through the tall iron gate. We were told to stay on the path and reluctantly allowed to jump rope; ball playing was forbidden, lest it roll irreverently among the ancient tombstones. It was a peculiar playground.

Finally, in second grade we were permitted to play among the older kids in the regular yard. It really was not very safe. In one disastrous game of 'crack the whip,' I was at the end of the long chain of children. The whip cracked and I fell to the ground, banging my head on the cement. I yelled loudly. The irritated teacher grumbled at me, "Oh, stop making such a fuss."

She reluctantly allowed me to lie down on the couch in the principal's office. "Maybe I should tell her I can't see," I thought, but was too timid. "She probably knows already; grownups know everything."

I lay on the couch watching the books on the shelves along the wall as they slowly emerged through a white fog. The principal poked her head through the door and demanded, "Well, are you feeling better now?"

"A little," I admitted. I wonder what the old battle-ax would have done if I had added, "I can see some of the books now."

Since I had recovered, I was told to go back to my classroom and the ongoing geography lesson. The teacher was explaining that the world was round and pointing to the location of tiny Denmark on the globe. As she spun the sphere to show other parts of the world, the room started to spin around me and I dramatically threw up at her feet.

They finally did what they should have done in the first place and called Mor. "The idiots just told me that Anne wasn't feeling well and I should come and take her home," she later told Far. "I came on my bike and couldn't leave it there, so Anne balanced on the seat while I pushed. I thought we'd never get home."

She brought me home and tucked me in bed. I slept and slept for what seemed weeks, to recover from my serious concussion.

∽

A lady came to our classroom once a week to teach us religion. The state religion is Lutheran, reformed and given its peculiarly Danish character by the same Bishop Gruntvig who changed the educational system and wrote so many beautiful hymns. Consequently, the stories of the Bible are part of the curriculum in public as well as private schools. Since, by law, there is freedom of religion, I suppose one could be excused from the class, but no one ever was. Our teacher was an evangelist and not satisfied with us merely learning stories.

"Put your heads down on your desks and listen; then God will speak to you," she commanded.

"God, who does she think she is to tell You what to do? You can talk to me later, whenever you feel like it," I mumbled into my folded arms, aiming my thoughts out the window towards the top of the spire of the Church of Our Savior where God surely lived. If I didn't like being told what to do, how must God feel?

I'm not sure whether my core of rebellious independence inside a conformist frame came from nature or nurture, but no one in my little family ever liked being told what to do. Mor and Far, through their example and their stories, taught me that although they definitely had high expectations of me, I should also think for myself.

I don't remember being unhappy at The Daughters' School, despite these unfortunate incidents. When, several years later, I became miserable, Mor decided it was time for me to go elsewhere. In fact, I don't remember much about school during those early years when the war and occupation were still a backdrop that could usually be ignored. Playing with friends in the yard and in the park was much more important to a child living By The Rampart.

THREE

Ulla

U lla and I were very best friends, meeting soon after the move to the new apartment building. Mor and I had gone down to the wading pond in the middle of the yard so I could get to know the many children. She sat down on the long bench to talk to the other mothers, as usual, getting perfect strangers to tell their stories. Ulla's mother walked by carrying the daily groceries and they struck up a conversation, swapping tales about their daughters.

"I found a new friend for you." Mor said as we went back upstairs to prepare dinner. "Ulla is a few years older than you, but very shy and full of imagination so you'll get along well."

Ulla and I didn't meet that day because she was home in bed with the measles. There must have been an epidemic among the children because shortly thereafter I caught them too. Mor had firm rules about bedrest after a fever: one day in bed after the temperature returned to normal, then half a day up, followed by a half-day outside. Those two days at the end were always very boring.

"Why don't we invite Ulla over to play? She can't get the measles again," Mor suggested, taking pity on my restlessness on the first-day-after-measles-fever.

"Play with an eight-year old! Three years older and in second grade!" I was too young to usually question that Mor knew best or to resent her arranging my life, but this time I was certain she was wrong. This would never work! Nevertheless, Ulla was invited and soon came holding her mother's hand.

She was taller than I, even thinner and her blond hair paler. She stared at me with slightly protruding blue eyes, as shy and tentative as I.

We were allowed to play in my parents' bedroom, I on my mother's bed since I was still supposed to rest. Mor went shopping, leaving us in the care of the new cleaning woman, Miss Loud. I don't think her name has any particular meaning in Danish, but we were scared of this stranger. We wanted our promised milk and cookies, but couldn't get up the nerve to call her from the kitchen. "*Kom Frøken Laud*—come Miss Loud," we whispered, then beat the rhythm of the syllables on the mattress: one long, two short, and a long. Breaking into hysterical giggles, we made this our secret signal.

Instantly we were best friends, bonded by our imagination and shyness. We became constant mates in the yard and ran back and forth between our apartments to play.

Our mothers had warned us not to open the door for strangers when home alone. The little peephole in the door was too high for us to reach without a chair and, anyway, one couldn't tell who was ringing the bell at the door at the entry below. So we always rang our secret signal on the door bell: 'one long, two short, and a long' now it came to mean: *Kom og luk op*— 'come and open up.'

Ulla, too, was an only child, living with her parents in an apartment several entries away. Its layout was mirror image to ours, but slightly larger since they had both a dining room and a master bedroom. Her room was the same as mine, just big enough for her bed and clothes chest. Her mother was even more protective of her than Mor was of me. Her father was an obscure figure, usually sitting quietly at his desk at one end of the living room. He was a civil engineer with a land reclamation project, located at the edge of the city and inactive during the war. He had had tuberculosis and was always afraid of infecting Ulla.

Like my family, Ulla's was very close. They made trick home movies, had Sunday picnics, and went to her grandparents' farm in the summer. Each Christmas her father gave her a chapter of his boyhood memoirs, typed and bound like a real book. I wanted to read his stories, but they were just for her family and not to be shared. Imagine our great surprise at the end of the war when we found out that this quiet man had been a member of the Underground. "Nothing heroic," he said. "Just paperwork." Here was another family secret that Ulla was not allowed to share with me; for good reason.

Ulla went to The Daughters' School nearby, the same one I was eventually to attend. She was not happy there, but her father said, "School is the natural enemy of the family," and so she stayed because they were all the same.

We gathered handfuls of snowberries and mixed them with orangy-red ones from a mountain ash. Red and white are the colors of the Danish flag, so this mixture was just the thing for the king's birthday parade downtown. We filled our shoulder bags to strew them at His Majesty's feet, but he was sick and couldn't leave the palace. We scattered berries with patriotic fervor anyway.

"Before the war, when the fountain in the Old Market Square wasn't turned off, they balanced gold balls on top of the water spouts on the king's birthday," Ulla told me. Imagine that: real gold balls. How could they balance on a water fountain?

Ulla's mother had made her a stuffed doll, about twelve inches tall with braids and a little cap, in the same calico fabric as the 'blouse' that was her upper body. Her name was Babsen. I had to have a Babsen too, but mine was store-bought and not as nice. These rag dolls became our alter egos, able to go where even skinny little girls couldn't. At night they canoed inside the radiators between our apartments so they could play together even when we were in bed.

We set a time, shortly after bedtime when we tapped our secret signal on the radiators. "The pipes conducts the sound between our rooms," we decided. If only we knew Morse code, we could send messages. I spent many hours imagining how we could string wire outside, from my window to hers, for a secret telephone. Why this would have been better than the normal telephone remains one of the mysteries of childhood.

"I can't play today because Mor and I are making Babsen's spring clothes," Ulla said one afternoon. I was very jealous of their fun project together and because her mother took my friend away for the afternoon.

When I saw the finished doll in her fresh new finery, I was deeply shocked. "You mean you've completely re-sown Babsen's body? A new head and face, too?" Was this really the same Babsen if most of her was new? How was one to know?

Best friends and two Babsens.

Kirsten was another friend who lived in our apartment complex, a year younger than Ulla, two years older than I. The three of us became frequent companions, a triangle with Ulla at the apex. We played outdoors in the courtyard as much as we could, in good weather and indifferent, summer and winter. Sometimes we played with the other girls in the yard. The boys usually went their own way, unless we joined forces for rare large group games. Traditional games went by an instinctive calendar: ball and jump rope in the fall, hopscotch in the spring, other games in the summer. In the spring, no sooner were we able to take off our rubber boots, hats, and hated long wool stockings than we were off to the hardware store for hopscotch supplies: chalk, broom handles, and hopscotch stones. The chalk was for drawing numbered game squares on the cement and the 'stones' were pale-colored glass disks about the size of a child's hand. They had a decoration incised on the top but were smooth on the bottom so they could slide along the cement. Although we sometimes played the game familiar to American children, consisting of a series of squares arranged in an airplane pattern, usually we played a Danish version. A large square is drawn on the cement and divided into nine numbered fields. A semi-circle is added at the top, numbered '10' and called 'Home.' Each player, in turn, balances on her right foot with the help of the broomstick then hop-kicks her stone just hard enough to make it slide into the square with the next number. She must then hop to that square, close to the stone, and repeat the process until reaching 'Home.' Great skill is required to land both stone and foot in the right square without either touching any of the lines. A misstep marks the end of the turn. Variations, including balancing without the broomstick, are added as skill improves with age.

In the fall we played with balls. Not group games like 'round ball'—that was for summer, but a competitive game of individual skill. The ball is tossed or batted with the hand in intricate patterns so that it bounces against the wall of a building and is caught. When the basic game is mastered, progressions are added. At the top level the game can be played with two or even three balls juggled simultaneously. I never could do these advanced versions. Since I was so much younger than Ulla and Kirsten, I was allowed to stick to the basic game.

On the rare occasions when we couldn't think of what to do, we had a game called 'idea.' We would twirl until we became so dizzy we fell to the ground. In this altered state of consciousness one of us would exclaim, "I am catching an idea," and a new fantasy would be hatched.

During the long, light, Danish summer evenings, we were allowed to play outside after dinner until bedtime, but during the winter we were supposed to come in at dusk. Since we weren't home from school until after 2 o'clock and the sun set as early as 4, there was not much time. I ran home, dumped my backpack in my room, changed to play clothes, and dashed downstairs and outside.

Mor stood by the door, tucking a sandwich into my hand as I streaked by. "And I rushed home from shopping downtown so I would be here for this?" she grumbled, but smiled to see me so happy.

We finally persuaded our mothers to let us stay outside until dinner time if we played under the street lamp by the bike racks. The tall lamp had a metal shade to keep the light from being seen from the air; part of the black-out regulations. The dimmed light made a magic spotlight on the pavement, sharply defined by the shade. In this little imaginary kingdom we eked out the remaining playtime until we heard a voice call, "Aan-neh" or "Uu-llaah" from a balcony above. We were supposed to keep track of the time by the big church clock because our mothers didn't consider it proper to yell from the balcony like fishwives, but we often forgot.

The pond in the middle of the apartment complex froze and it was time to skate. Our skates were fastened to our shoes by little keys. As my feet grew, the skates were lengthened by an adjustment and then tightening a bolt. By the last winter of the war, they were at the limit of their extension and kept falling off. Although we could sometimes get new shoes, there were no ration cards for skates.

"Hey kids, get off the ice. It's not safe," an intruding policeman scolded. We all clustered around and finally persuaded him that this was not like the deep moat outside the rampart, but just an itty bitty wading pond. At most, our ankles could get wet; drowning was impossible. Some grownups are so stupid.

As we became older we were allowed to go outside the yard to the rampart park and along the moat that was the outer ring of the old fortifications around the city. This moat was not just a shallow ditch as one might see around a castle, but a deep semi-circular lake, wider than the canals of the city. Neither was the rampart a little dirt mound, but a massive hill, as tall as the apartment building. The park was extensive, with footpaths winding through trees and bushes, onto the top of the rampart, and down along the water. A large playground with a wading area at the edge of the moat was a favorite spot. At the northern end were the army barracks, now billets for the occupying German soldiers. We didn't need to be reminded to stay well away from the massive rolls of barbed wire and the pacing guards with machine guns.

On top of the rampart hill, exposed to the wind from all directions, were the remains of *Lille Mølle*— 'the Little Mill.' I suppose it was called that in contrast to the 'Big Mill' further out on the island where we had lived on Big Mill Road. It wasn't exactly little and certainly not a ruin. The cluster of buildings had been converted into a house by removing the big mill-wings and the rotating top of the tower. There lived our fourth friend, Birgit, with her parents and older brother in lonely but splendid isolation with the whole park to themselves at night. The base of the tower made a magnificent living room, like the main room of an ancient castle keep. An indoor balcony circled the room, the walls lined with large bookcases and doors to second floor studies and bedrooms.

Birgit's father was a well-known lawyer and president of the Danish-American Society. To be famous was dangerous during the German occupation, so the family lived very quiet, obscure lives. We were not supposed to talk about who they were or notice when her father was home or away. 'Away' may have been a euphemism for illicit trips to Sweden, or perhaps he was simply hiding in the country.

Birgit went to a different school and could not always play with us because she was busy with piano and dancing lessons, but when we went to the park we checked to see if she was home.

They had a lovely walled garden, ripe with geraniums. We picked the colorful flower petals and put them in little bottles of water. Red barberries and white snow berries completed the concoction. Ulla and I took our treasures to my room and closed the casement storm windows. Mor had glued black-out paper to the glass so the room was quite dark, but a ray of light came in through a crack and hit the window sill. Kneeling on my bed, we shook the bottles to make the colored bits dance in the spotlight: two blond heads together, telling tales of a botanical ballet.

A few weeks later, we visited Birgit again to play with the rest of the magic bottles that we had saved in her shed. Rot had set in and turned the beautiful colored bits to brown goo. The stench was unbelievable. To this day I hold my breath when planting geraniums in my window box.

The rampart park had wonderful old trees leaning over the moat. We hung from a branch, daringly swinging out over the water until a park policeman chased us away. Was he worried about us or the trees? Both seemed perfectly safe to us. Grown-ups always spoil the fun for no good reason.

One day Ulla and I decided to visit Far at the lab so I could show her the experimental animals. The State Serum Institute was a large facility of research laboratories, the central clinical laboratory for all of Denmark which produced vaccines and sera for treatment of infections. The grounds were extensive, housing the main building of laboratories, the director's magnificent residence, and the animals. It was a veritable zoo with little white mice and big rats in glass jars, guinea pigs, mink and white rabbits in outdoor cages, and even stables with cows (for small pox vaccine) and horses (for anti-tetanus serum). I often went there with Far on week-ends, to check his experiments.

Mor and I also visited together, but she was reluctant to go because she feared she might run into Crown Princess Ingrid. "Then I have to curtsy, and she's a year younger than I," she would explain.

The director of the Institute was a famous man and a close friend of the king and the royal family. Crown Prince Frederick and Ingrid liked to play tennis on the Institute courts, hence it was not unusual to see them there. Even Mor's usual snobbery was too socialistic to be impressed by royalty.

The Institute was too far for me to go there by myself, but Ulla was old enough and we were allowed to go together. We went out of the courtyard by the old yellow city gatehouse and crossed busy *Torvegade*— 'Market Street'. Then we walked through the rampart park along the lake of the old wide moat. This was not the part of the park where we usually played because it was on the other side of the big street that formed the boundary for most of our excursions. To get to work, Far bicycled down *Torvegade*, which bridged the moat and then circled around to the wide avenue, *Amager Boulevard*, where the Institute still lies. Walking through the park was a shortcut. There was a funny long and narrow footbridge across the moat. It floated right on top of the water and was very scary to walk on because it bobbed up and down with every step. In the middle was a large gate that was sometimes locked to prevent crossing; why it was locked, I couldn't figure out. What else was the bridge for but for people to cross?

On the other side, we crossed Amager Boulevard and approached the gate house of the Institute grounds. Knowing exactly what to do because I had watched Mor so often, I confidently walked up to the guard and said, "I am Fru Doktor Ipsen, here to visit . . . No, that's not right!" I halted in confusion.

"I didn't think so," said the amused guard, "But you may visit your father anyway."

We were interested in nature and began collecting leaves and feathers. We sketched a bone, convinced it was a duck's cranium. "That rounded part must be the top of the head," I said, pointing to the ball joint. I knew all about nature from my amateur naturalist grandfather who had taught me.

My uncle was visiting from out of town and came to inspect our great find—he also knew about such things from his father. "I think it's just an old leg bone from a roast that a dog dragged out here. It seems a little large for a duck," he chuckled. I crossed out the drawing in my sketch book, deflated by reality and embarrassed by my naïveté.

One day we found some funny little round rubber disks and they, too, went into the collecting bag.

"Ulla's mother called, she was very angry to find used condoms on her dining room table," Mor said, torn between amusement and upset. "Do you even know what they are?"

She was at a loss as to how to explain to the much younger Anne why these were not suitable objects for nature collecting. A light bulb went on in my head. Mor and I had been at the pharmacy and a man had asked for something. The pharmacist had demonstrated how to put them on using his thumb, as Mor hustled me out of the store. That's what they were for—infected thumbs. Ugh!

Ulla was a talented artist. Her mother bought large square sketch-books and had them cut in half for her drawings. She drew cartoons of a little boy called Balli and his fantastic adventures with his little friends.

I, too, had to have sketchbooks. Mor liked being able to save my drawings, treasuring the completed books in the middle drawer of

Far's antique oak desk. The older Anne drew landscapes, but in those early efforts, I also had to have imaginary children in imaginary adventures or, sometimes, stories about my life. I was not as talented as Ulla and my derivative cartoon characters were stiff on awkward legs. I had trouble remembering that the sequence of frames was supposed to go from left to right and down the page. I later added numbers to clarify the jumble, usually from right to left, bottom to top. When I learned to write, I added obscure legends and dialogue with atrocious spelling.

"Advertisement for the middle," reads a colorful picture of a wall-hanging with flowers along the border. It is in the center of the book; the fold of the paper and the staples cut the picture in half. Ulla had temporarily run out of ideas one day when she was inspired by that important landmark to draw a special picture. I had to skip several pages so that I too could commemorate the middle of my book. We drew with much giggling and sharing of colored pencils. We didn't have crayons, but little flat boxes of 'Viking' pencils. According to the cover, one could use a paint brush and water to smooth out and intensify the color, but we didn't usually do that.

"Look, Ulla's picture is in *Politiken*," Mor said one day in surprise. The newspaper-publishing house had run a children's drawing contest and she had won first prize. There she was in her Girl Scout uniform.

"Why didn't you tell me?" I complained to Ulla.

"At first I was afraid I might not win; then I wanted to surprise you," she answered.

I was very proud of my friend but disappointed she hadn't wanted to share her daring with me beforehand. I felt she had held something of herself back because she thought me too young; by then I was nine to her mature twelve.

Soon her little illustrated book of Balli's adventures in kindergarten was published. A couple of years later it was joined by *Ballis Juledrøm*— 'Balli's Christmas Dream'.

"Mor, why can't I be a Girl Scout? You were when you were a little girl."

"Scouts are for children who don't have a family place to go to in the summer, so they go to scout camp. We have our cabin at the lake, so you don't need the scouts."

"But Ulla goes to the farm in the summer, and camping sounds like fun."

Mor had told me how she used to stand at the foot of her parents' bed on Sunday mornings to remind her father that she needed a 10 øre coin for the weekly dues. Her unspoken message was that scouting was for poor children like her and was therefore beneath a doctor's daughter. Arguments that Ulla wasn't poor were best left unsaid because Mor could not be budged once her mind was made up.

One evening, Kirsten, Birgit, and I were playing at Ulla's apartment and decided to form a secret club.

"Why don't you call it K.U.B.A. from your initials?" Ulla's mother suggested.

"Here's the flag Far used to put on the car when he made emergency house calls," said Mor when I told her of our new project. "That can be your club flag."

The little pale yellow triangle looked grand with 'KUBA' drawn in big letters and four colors. We met every Saturday night from 6:30 until 8:30, taking turns being hostess. Birgit couldn't always come, but when she did, her father came to pick her up afterward because of the dark walk home to the mill. Other times, Ulla's or my father walked her home. Kirsten's father didn't live at home, so when it was her turn there were usually only three of us because there was no one to walk Birgit home. The final year of the war, Birgit couldn't come at all because there was an evening curfew; if caught outside one could get shot. The remaining three of us lived in different entries of the apartment complex, but they were connected underground by a dark and rat-infested basement, so we continued to meet. I used to cling to Far's hand along the way as I watched the half-naked workers stoking the central furnace and the rats scurrying away into the darkness beyond the light from the few bare bulbs in the ceiling.

One Saturday night, the telephone rang. "Where is Anne?" Ulla's mother demanded.

Mor and I had completely forgotten about the KUBA meeting. Far was out and the two of us were making Danish pancakes. I had received a set of tiny cast iron pots and pans for my birthday, and we were cozily experimenting with making miniature crepes. I was flipping them in the air with great élan.

"Ulla is in tears and won't talk to you," Mor said. She held out the telephone so I could hear Ulla having hysterics in the background. Mor and I had been having such fun; couldn't they have called earlier, before it was too late for me to go?

This magical friendship continued despite ups and downs and despite the intensification of the fighting-war around Denmark. Although we were always aware of the war and the restrictions of the occupation, we seldom allowed them to intrude on our private, nearly perfect world.

FOUR

Frit Danmark

Iwent to get the morning milk and fresh baked rolls at the front door. There was a little compartment for small deliveries built into the door, but I had to go out on the landing to open it and reach the milk. I never could understand why it was there, but supposed the architects thought it more elegant to have the bottles discretely tucked inside these little compartments rather than to have them clutter up the landings. I felt it would have been easier if there had been an opening to the compartment inside the apartment as well, so one didn't have to open the front door to fetch the bottles. The door also had a mail slot. In those days, Danish mailmen wore bright red uniforms, biked their route, and delivered the mail twice a day all the way upstairs to our fourth floor apartment. The mail and the milk usually arrived early in the morning, before I dressed and left for school.

"*Frit Danmark* is here!" I yelled. A thin bunch of papers had come in through the slot and were lying on the floor.

"Not so loud," Far protested. "The newspaper is printed by the Underground, and we and the person who delivered it will get in a lot of trouble if the Germans hear you."

"What's the Underground?" What an odd word, I thought. Copenhagen, then as now, had no subway, but I imagined tunnels and caves under the city where these newspapers were printed and other secret activities took place.

This newspaper and another one called *Information* gave us news that was censored by the Germans from the regular papers. *Information* was so well-known that after the war it became a commercial newspaper, joining the older *Berlingske Tidene* and *Politiken*.

The papers were not always placed in the mail slot, but sometimes little stacks would be left on the window sills in our entry. Coming down the stairs one dark afternoon, I heard someone running down the steps and found a little pile of papers at the next landing. Who was the invisible messenger? It was better not to know. I ran back up the stairs, waving the latest news. There was an elevator, but children were supposed to use the stairs and not waste power. The lights were on a timer and on just long enough for the usual wait for the elevator but too briefly for me to make it up the three flights of stairs. I ran up as fast as my young legs could go. I lost the race again and had to run the last few steps in the dusk.

There were so many secrets. We whispered stories and rumors of the latest sabotage and tricks played on the Germans; possibly, some were even true. During the first few years, the German army was just there to 'protect' us from invasion by the British. The occupation duty was considered light, and soldiers were sent to Denmark for R&R from fighting at the front.

A friend told us of overhearing two German soldiers on the streetcar say, "Isn't this a lovely little country *der Führer* has found for us?" Did they think Hitler was a Moses and Denmark the land of milk and honey?

The soldiers found the food fantastic and rushed to the bakeries to buy cakes, the more whipped cream the better. Sometimes they bought just the whipped cream.

Gradually, the Danes became more unfriendly, rebelling in the only safe way by avoiding the soldiers whenever possible.

Mor taught me some subtle lessons on our shopping trips. "Let's wait here a minute," she said one day on the way to buying bread, stopping half-way down the block when she saw two officers going into our bakery. They always walked in pairs like green-clad unholy nuns. Through the window of the bakery, I could see the other customers quickly leave. We all waited outside.

The clerk placed a piece of cardboard on a large square of white tissue paper. Then she put four cakes in the middle and folded the paper loosely over the top so as not to crush the cream. "Værsgo—'Here you are'," she would have said, polite but cool. Out they came, shiny black boots, green uniforms, military bearing, one of them carefully balancing the white package on the palm of his hand like a waiter. We waited with the little crowd until they were down the street before going in to buy our bread.

Soon the soldiers stopped going to the bakeries, disconcerted by the frigid courtesy, the emptying stores. Then the whipped cream disappeared anyway, the cream needed to make rationed butter. Sugar and flour also became rationed and our coupons were not squandered on cakes and cookies.

There were other incidents, seemingly innocent enough at the time, but puzzling to a young child. I tucked them away in my mind to be reasoned out later. One day, Mor and I got on the No. 2 streetcar to return home from downtown. The streetcars had open platforms at the front and back for standing passengers while sliding doors separated these open areas from the central compartment with seats. As usual, I was fascinated by the driver who stood on the front platform, turning a brass handle on the dashboard before him to accelerate or slow the car. At the end of the line, he would lift the handle, walk to the other end, insert the handle, and start the car in the other direction. What an ingenious system.

Two soldiers climbed on ahead of us. They slid the door open and sat down. It was the end of the afternoon and nearly all the seats were taken, but there were just two seats left for us. Mor said softly, "Hold on tight, we'll stay out here on the platform."

"Why?" I asked.

"Shh, I'll explain later."

By the next stop, the compartment was almost empty but the platforms at the front and back were packed with standing passengers. Eventually, the soldiers got off and the rest of us sat down. 'Passive resistance,' we called it; an amazingly effective way of quietly and safely protesting the occupation. Soon soldiers did not sit down on streetcars; they preferred standing in the cold air on the platform to the chilly reception inside the compartment.

By the end of the war, soldiers only appeared in larger troops, marching in the streets, guarded on both sides by more soldiers with submachine guns at the ready. "Why do they carry guns like that?" I wondered, but figured out that the guards were there to shoot in case one of the soldiers decided to run away. I thought it was sad for them not to be trusted and to have to be kept in line by a machine gun. I made up my own explanations when puzzled and often they were not quite right; it didn't occur to me that the guards were there to protect the soldiers against attack by the Underground.

The resentment of the people deepened. Soldiers and officials continued to be harassed in more and more ingenious ways.

One day, Far chuckled and showed me *Berlingske Tidene*. "Here's the ad I heard about at work, announcing a big sale with ridiculously low prices. The phone number is the one for Gestapo headquarters. They say the switchboard was swamped all morning with bargain hunters. The editor had to call up the Germans and apologize." Then Far had to explain the joke to me.

Another time he told us, "Two members of the Underground were supposed to blow up a building downtown. A man came walking along the sidewalk just as they had placed the explosives. They attempted to hurry the man along, but he thought they were just trying to annoy him. Finally, in exasperation they yelled: 'Damn it, run; the building is going to explode!'" Normally, Mor didn't allow swearing in front of me, but a funny story was a funny story.

The family photo album has a snapshot of me sitting at our small spinet piano, a big white bow in my hair. I wanted to learn to play like Far, so he started to teach me the names of the notes and where to find them on the keyboard. In a book of my drawings, I am sitting at the piano, Far standing beside me. The view is from the side so that I wouldn't have to draw all the keys.

"Be," the balloon next to his mouth says, as he dictated the key I was supposed to play. "Anne is learning to play the piano from Far," says the title at the top of the page. Every word, except 'Anne,' 'Far,' and 'to' is misspelled. I was learning to both spell and to play.

A chandelier with four arms hangs from the ceiling. The trick of how to draw something coming straight toward me was an unsolved problem, the rules of perspective drawing learned much later. On the right side of the piano, I drew the dining room table with a chair carefully pushed underneath it. "Put your chair back under the table," Mor always had to remind me.

Floating above the piano is an awkward sketch of Hokusai's 'The Wave.' A Japanese physician visiting before the war had given the print to Far. It always hung on the wall in back of the piano, so it belonged in my picture.

When I was much younger, I had trouble understanding 'the Wave.' "That's a picture of my mother's evening gown," I explained to one of my friends. Mor had a beautiful gown of silvery-gray colored brocade; the foam on the wave looked like lace to me, the wave like the swirl of the skirt. The frightened faces peering over the edge of the boat and Mount Fuji in the background were too abstract for me to understand.

I realized that my explanation was not quite right, so I asked Far, "Tell me again about that picture."

Mor's gown had a story of its own. She wore it to a party and stood too close to the fireplace. A spark burned some holes along one edge. "I can't give you the full replacement value for the dress," the insurance adjuster said, but handed Mor a large check.

The skirt was very full, so a tuck along one seam took care of the damage. "Six meters of fabric in the skirt," Mor claimed.

"Look what I found and bought with the insurance check," she said a few weeks later, returning from town with a lovely antique English silver teapot.

After that, we pointed to the teapot instead of the picture and said, "That's Mor's evening gown."

Mor decided I needed a regular piano teacher, so once a week she took me some blocks away to a dingy studio. While Mor waited on the couch, the dumpy teacher, wearing a dress of dark blue serge, towered over me as I perched on a little stool. She pointed to the notes with a long stick and called out, "Do, re, mi . . ." accompanied by mysterious hand signs. I could never make the connection between these mysterious lessons and the Mozart I wanted so badly to learn to play.

I finally balked. "I think someone younger might be better," Mor decided, not wanting to discourage my initial enthusiasm. "I'll ask Mrs. Koppel for the name of her daughter's piano teacher."

The brothers Koppel were famous musicians. One was a concert pianist and composer, and the other played the viola. The two families lived in our apartment building: the viola-playing brother, his violinist wife, and their small daughter on the seventh floor above us; the pianist and their slightly older daughter in another entry. Fru Holm-Johansen was the older girl's teacher and may formerly have been Mr. Koppel's pupil. Once a week she went to their apartment to teach the daughter and could then very conveniently come to give me my lesson. The war had postponed her career as a concert pianist. I loved to watch her hands, soft and limber, the fingers bouncing on the keys as if they were pulled up by rubber bands. I thought she was absolutely beautiful. Besides, she let me play *real* music, with both hands together. My first piece was a lovely folk song with an Alberti base in the left hand. It was almost as good as playing Mozart.

"Where can she be?" we wondered. It was time for my lesson and Fru Holm-Johansen was very late. She finally arrived white and shaking with fright. Her husband was an officer in the Danish army, or had been. Now they were both in the Underground, responsible for collecting information and keeping records of collaborators. They had been warned of a raid on their office and had escaped by bike with all the records, just in time. She probably wasn't allowed to tell us, but she was very upset, and Mor always had a way of getting people to talk. What a terrible life. They had a small son who stayed at home with his grandmother during the day, but the family spent every night together in a different place. I wondered if they slept in the underground tunnels.

"We don't have a lot of room, but if you need a place for a night or two, just let us know," Mor offered.

"I'll find out if that's all right," my teacher said, gratefully.

The next week she told Mor, "I'm afraid we can't stay here. Your name's on the Gestapo black list."

What frightening news. The Gestapo kept lists of suspects, and Far was probably on it because he was a physician. Many doctors, students, and other members of the intelligencia were known to be activists and therefore suspected by the Gestapo. I had heard that, in retaliation for an act of sabotage, the Gestapo had gone to the nearest hospital, picked out a group of doctors and nurses at random, and shot them; I worried that they were going to come and round us up. Were we going to have to sleep in a different place every night?

Far had a telephone call. "This is Niels Bohr. My family and I need to be vaccinated. Would you mind coming to the house on Sunday? Bring the family for tea."

"He asked me to be his personal physician because of his old friendship with my father," Far explained to us. "I get the impression he is planning to leave the country and is using the invitation to tea as camouflage for the preparations. But wait until you see their house!"

Niels Bohr was Denmark's most outstanding scientist and had won the Nobel Prize many years earlier for his theory about the orbital structure of the hydrogen atom. The Carlsberg Fund (of Danish beer fame) built the Bohr Institute for him, a Mecca for physicists around the world. The Carlsberg founder had built a grand mansion for himself and his family right on the brewery grounds. In his will he had left it as an 'honors residence' for the use of an outstanding Dane, at that time Niels Bohr.

He and my grandfather had been contemporaries at the university and were good friends. There were four of them: my grandfather, Ole Chievitz, Niels Bjerrum, and Niels Bohr. My grandfather and Chievitz became surgeons, Bjerrum a chemist, and Bohr a physicist. They often met on Sundays to sail or go for walks in the country. On the Sunday after the announcement that Niels Bohr had won the Nobel Prize in Physics, they met for their usual hike. They walked all morning in the beautiful woods of *Dyrehaven*. This forest, located just north of Copenhagen, was formerly the king's hunting preserve. During the last century, it was given to the people and is now a huge public park of ancient trees, roaming deer, restaurants, and even an amusement park.

The conversation was lively, as usual, but no one said a word about the great honor bestowed on Bohr. Finally they went to their favorite inn to have lunch, consuming their usual generous tray of open-faced sandwiches and beer, followed by schnapps and cigars. Still, no congratulations.

They were about to divide the bill, as was their custom, when Chievitz or Bjerrum, I cannot remember which, said dryly, "Since Bohr is so rich, the least he can do is to pay the whole bill." That was all that was said.

Bjerrum was a character and became a famous chemist. Some years after Bohr had been named, there was a rumor that Bjerrum had been nominated for the Nobel Prize, as well. He was at a scientific meeting the day the announcement was expected when an usher came up to him and said, "You have a phone call from Stockholm."

"Never mind, tell them you couldn't find me," said Bjerrum, knowing full well what 'a phone call from Stockholm' meant and ducking into an obscure corner of the meeting hall.

Promising the flustered usher that he would take care of the problem, the chairman of the meeting went to the microphone at the podium and announced loudly, "Niels Bjerrum has a telephone call from Stockholm. Please take it at the front desk."

Bjerrum answered reluctantly, but had the nerve to turn down the prize. He explained that he didn't want the honor because the money would be so heavily taxed that it wasn't worth the fuss. Scandalous. From that day, and even to-day, foundation awards are not taxed in Denmark. But Bjerrum's name is not on the list of past Nobel laureates.

Ole Chievitz had known my grandfather from elementary school. He was a famous surgeon, chief of the Finsen Institute Hospital, a freedom fighter in Finland, and, as it turned out, a hero and leader in the Danish Underground.

Grandfather had some friends.

So, on that Sunday, with great anticipation, we took the streetcar to the northern part of Copenhagen and Bohr's house. Far carried his medical bag that he hardly ever used because he worked at the lab and never saw patients. We got off near the harbor and could see the huge cranes for loading the beer crates onto ships. They were a strange backdrop for the grand Carlsberg mansion.

Mrs. Bohr was a gracious hostess. After tea and inoculations, Bohr gave us a tour of the house and gardens. He was like a child showing off his toys. "Look at this, I'll turn on the water so you can see the waterfall. We have to keep it off to save power." He bounded up to the top of some boulders and showed me how the graceful little Japanese stream flowed through the garden.

"Come into the conservatory and see the banana and orange trees," he said enthusiastically. "This little orange is coming along nicely." The conservatory was a large glass house filled with huge palm trees and other tropical plants. In the center was a tiled water fountain surrounded by patio chairs. It looked like something from a fairy castle.

"Let me turn on the fountain," Bohr continued. "Here's a Ping-Pong ball for each of us. If we are very careful we can balance them on top of the jets of water. There, isn't that marvelous?"

"Is that like the gold balls they used to balance on the water fountain on the king's birthday?" I asked the great physicist.

"Look at the two of them; it's not clear who is having more fun!" said Mrs. Bohr, fondly.

We must have been a sight: the large teddy bear with a huge head playing with the awed string bean of a little girl.

Soon after that Sunday, we heard that Niels Bohr had gone to Sweden and from there, by light plane, to England. They gave him an oxygen mask that didn't fit properly over his large head. To everyone's horror, he was unconscious when they landed in England. "I had such a peaceful nap," he later said.

Part of the precious cargo was a case of beer bottles filled with 'heavy water' smuggled out of a plant in Norway. Heavy water contains a radioactive isotope of hydrogen and was, at the time, thought to be crucial for the construction of an atomic bomb. The Germans had built a plant in Norway because of the easy access to the huge amount of hydroelectric power needed to produce the isotope.

"I didn't know how to hide it, so I put it in the wine cellar with the beer," Bohr told Far later.

From England he went on to Los Alamos in New Mexico to visit the rest of the atomic scientists. He traveled incognito as 'Mr. Brown.' On the train he happened to meet an acquaintance. "Hello, Professor Bohr. What are you doing here?" she said.

"My name isn't Bohr, but how are you, Mrs. Hansen?" said the absent-minded professor to the horror of his secret service escort.

Of course, I knew none of these upcoming events that Sunday and would have understood little of their import. Years later, when I heard the tales of the atomic bomb and studied physics, I remembered the famous man who loved children and had been so kind and full of fun. The greatest irony was that this scientific and humanitarian genius was Jewish (on his mother's side). He had delayed his departure as long as possible, feeling an obligation to stay in his country and use his influence as part of the Resistance. If he had not been needed as a physicist for the development of the atomic bomb, would he have stayed in Denmark and been sent to concentration camp? Or would even the Germans have been impressed by his Nobel Prize?

A family lived on the floor below us. They had an older boy and a little girl with whom I sometimes played. I stood on the balcony one

Saturday morning and watched them walking out of our entry, all dressed up. The boy was wearing all black and a man's hat. I thought it looked very strange, a man's hat on a boy.

"He is thirteen and today he will to be confirmed; they call it *Bar Mitzvah*," Mor explained. "He's wearing the hat to show that now he is a man." She knew all the happenings in our entry.

This was the first time I knew anyone who wasn't Lutheran. An explanation must have followed about how the family was Jewish, but I don't remember anything but that hat. After a while they moved away. Perhaps they left the country in time to avoid the troubles to come.

The best stories in the Underground newspapers were about King Christian X. The Germans raised the swastika flag on a government building. "Take that down, or a Danish soldier will pull it down," said the king.

"If he does that he will be shot!"

"That Danish soldier will be *me*," said the king. The flag came down.

An order went out that Danish Jews were to wear yellow stars on their coats. The next morning, the king went on his usual ride around the city, wearing a large, conspicuous star on his uniform. By nightfall, every Dane was wearing a yellow star.

"Jews are Danes like all my people; Germany will be held responsible for the safety of each of them," said the king. A bargain was struck, the Danish Jews were not to be harmed. That deal held for a time, but finally succumbed to Hitler's demand for a 'final solution.'

During the summer of 1943, the fiction of Denmark as a happy protectorate became untenable and no longer useful. The Underground was more and more active, bombing the railway tracks on the cross-country routes, to prevent shipment of food and machinery to Germany. Factory workers producing war materiel for shipping to the front went on strike. King Christian was under house arrest at the palace and could no longer ride in his city. In Norway, which unlike Denmark had fiercely fought the initial occupation, the king escaped before the country fell and Vidkun Quisling became the puppet head of the collaborating government; his name synonymous with 'traitor.' We heard stories of the terrible treatment of the Norwegians, the lack of food, the impounded radios, and arrest of Jews. The dark threat used by the German occupation government was that if Denmark refused to cooperate 'Norwegian conditions' would be imposed on us as well. The Danes did not want a Quisling and a compromise government was elected by over ninety-five percent of the electorate. By August, the members of this Danish parliament refused a German ultimatum which included arrest of hostages, banning of public gatherings, and a death penalty for sabotage. They had had enough of cooperation and resigned *en masse*.

The internal affairs of the country continued to be run by the civil service bureaus; the political leadership came from the Freedom Council, the top organization of the Underground. They had railed throughout the war not only against the German occupation, but against what they considered the shameful collaboration of the government. Surprisingly, although freedom became more restricted and more shortages developed, near normalcy was maintained. The German occupation leadership realized that increasing the pressure could result in full-scale rebellion. Germany could not afford to divert a larger occupation force from the front and desperately needed the food and materiel that Denmark was supplying.

The German army commander imposed martial law, interred the army, and decided that an early evening curfew would help them keep control. The Danes treasure the long summer evenings. The nights are very short and the nightingale's singing is so loud one can hardly sleep. Many working people own or rent little plots of land outside the city where they grow vegetables and flowers, or simply spend the summer evenings enjoying their beer. An early curfew was not acceptable. "Enough" factory workers said and walked off their jobs. The country closed down. Fortunately, Mor and I were in the country, but Far commuted to work every day. He managed to catch one of the last trains out of Copenhagen.

The Gestapo eventually gave in, but by late September 1943, at Hitler's insistence, they made their big mistake. The order went out that the Danish Jews were to be rounded up during the High Holy Days in early October and sent to concentration camps, as they already had been in Germany and other occupied countries. The assumption was that a hidden anti-Semitism would finally emerge among the Danes, and the 'Final Solution' would be greeted with relief or at least acceptance. A German official leaked the order, whether out of decency or to avoid complete disaster, I am not sure. The warning spread very quickly. In amazing concert and with much individual heroism, all but a very small fraction of those Danes who also happened to be Jews were hidden, helped to the coast outside the city, and brought by boat eight miles across the Sound to Sweden.

"The Koppels went to Sweden in a rowboat last night," said a playmate; the yard was full of news and rumors. These famous musicians escaping in a little row boat? I thought of the little Koppel girl on the seventh floor above us in the entry and wondered if she had cried. Was she one of the little ones they had to inject with morphine to keep her quiet and safe for the trip? I worried about the older daughter of the other Koppel family, my rival with whom I shared my adored piano teacher. Was she safe too?

By the end of the day, the name had been changed on their doors and a new family moved in. All that the two Koppel families owned was kept safe. When they came back after the war, a year-and-a-half-later, everything was in place; the plants had even been watered.

Similar stories were told all over the country. There was a spontaneous conspiracy. The Danish police were supposed to help round up the Jews; instead they helped organize the great escape. The king was right: they were Danes, and one helps the neighbors.

Many people were amazed that anyone could think otherwise; some had never heard of Jews, perhaps confusing the term with 'Jutes'—the inhabitant of the peninsula of Jylland. The young son of one of Far's friends was puzzled. "I'm very worried," he said. "I hear they've taken the Jutes. I'm from Fyn; are we next?"

My friend Kirsten lived with her mother, sister, and younger brother about four entries away in the same building. The mother was a pharmacist, divorced or separated from the father who was an army officer. One day she came home and was surprised to find a strange name on her door. The manager came by and explained, "I thought we should change the name plate, just in case the Gestapo gets the idea of looking for your husband here."

The Gestapo tried to recoup their failure to capture most of the Jews and, in a devastating raid, they rounded up the police and sent them to concentration camp. Only the under-trained *Civil Beskyttelse* (*C.B.*)— 'auxiliary police' remained to keep order. The C.B. corps was originally formed so that young men, called by the universal draft to serve in the now dissolved military, could still perform their civic duty. In street language they were called 'foals' because their orders and training had consisted of following right behind a policeman as a foal trails behind its dam.

It became a matter of pride among us children to obey every traffic law, crossing the street only with the light. "We'll show them!" we said. As children we could do little but did our best to fight back using 'passive resistance.' Of course, as scarcities developed, some people took advantage of the lack order. We had to drag our bicycles up the three flights of stairs onto the back balcony to keep them from being stolen. To hamper communications, the telephone system was closed down for all but emergency calls. I couldn't use the phone to call Ulla. Mor figured out that she could reach Far by calling the central exchange and say she was calling Dr. Ipsen.

The summer of civic disorder and the escape of the Jews in the fall was a watershed in the Danish understanding of the true meaning of the occupation. Before that time the Underground had been largely uncoordinated, working in isolated little groups. By August the Resistance movement had grown larger and become more effective while the conscience of the people slowly woke. Until then, the general cooperation had worked well for both sides: in return for shipments of food and manufactured goods to Germany, the Danish civilian government remained in place and life was relatively orderly. Civilian order meant that the Germans needed few occupation troops in Denmark; the bulk could be used to fight at the Russian front. Then there were the strikes, escalating sabotage, the resignation of the government, and the order to transport the Danish Jews to concentration camp. The need to help the Jews escape brought the members of the Resistance together into an organized structure: a hierarchy of three-person cells, deliberately isolated for security, but with a common purpose and strategy. At the top was the increasingly powerful Freedom Council. The various groups had different origins: some were political, such as communistic, and others purely patriotic. Remarkably, past rivalries were buried and became unimportant.

The spontaneous rescue of the Jews supported by the effective organization of the Resistance leaders was the wake-up call. It was as if the Danes said with one voice, "Now wait a minute; this is not right, this was not the agreement!" Life-as-usual was recognized as an illusion and there was great moral clarity. The heroes were well-sung; the bad guys wore green uniforms.

"56-20 extra," Mor told the operator on the Taga telephone exchange. We had a dial telephone, but after you dialed the exchange, you had to give the number to the operator. The 'extra' at the end of the number was because it was a party line.

Moster Rigmor—Aunt Rigmor—was Mor's mother's sister. Mor called her almost every day. She was a large motherly woman married to a master bricklayer, and often came to our place to help Mor with the housework and baby-sit for me. Her husband had trouble getting work since not much construction was being done, or perhaps he had reached retirement age. Mor would discretely leave an envelope of money to help Moster.

Moster and her husband had no children of their own, but her nephew, Vesti, had lived with them when he was little. His parents (Mor's other aunt and her husband) had emigrated to New York sometime during the 1930's. While they were getting established, they left Vesti with Moster Rigmor but as soon as they had enough money, they sent for him to join them in White Plains. Moster Rigmor missed him very badly and talked about him constantly. I was very jealous and hoped she talked about me as much to others; I thought it quite dreadful that parents could leave their child, even with someone as nice as Moster.

I was down in the yard playing after school, as usual. Moster was in the apartment while Mor was in town. There was a loud banging on the neighbor's door and then a quiet knock on our back door to the kitchen balcony, which we shared with them. We didn't know the older couple that lived there very well, except that they had a very loud parrot called 'Ricard'—a fact he announced to the world frequently and loudly, with a hoarse screech.

Moster opened the balcony door, puzzled. It was hardly the usual place for us to receive company. "The Gestapo is at our front door. If they knock on yours, please don't let them in," whispered the neighbor lady.

When Mor came home, Moster Rigmor and the neighbor were shakily drinking *ersatz* coffee made from chicory. "They banged and banged, but we just pretended no one was home," they told Mor. "After a while, we went to the window and saw two officers leaving the entry. Just then they looked up and saw us looking down at them. So stupid we were. They turned right around and marched back up the stairs. We had to let them in. They searched everything, both here and at the neighbors, but finally they went away."

As usual I had missed all the action. Just think, I was right down there playing in the yard. What were they looking for? Perhaps they were just suspicious because our neighbor had been knighted by the king. He was a 'Knight of Dannebrog' and must be a *real* hero.

There in Far's desk was a stack of old *Frit Danmark* which the Gestapo never saw. What would have happened to us if they had found them? Or did they have more serious things to worry about than a few homemade newspapers?

FIVE

Oldemor

The effort to help the Danish Jews escape in the fall of 1943 was a watershed in the occupation. Before then, we could pretend that the horrors of war did not really touch us; after that, we could no longer ignore that we were all involved. We had had a vague feeling of shame that Denmark did not resist the initial occupation. Now, repressed shame was replaced by a combination of pride and fear: pride that as a country we were standing up to the enemy, and fear because we didn't know what might happen as a consequence. My awareness of the tensions also increased as I became old enough to understand the changes and abnormalities of this strange life: in the midst of war but yet removed. The horror of what was happening to the Jews touched me because of the story of Oldemor and her sister-in-law.

Oldemor was my great-grandmother on my father's side. She lived across town by *Søerne*, a chain of three small lakes just beyond the northwestern part of the old fortifications around the city. They were originally the reservoirs for the city's water supply, but have long since been civilized, bounded on all sides by straight walking paths and stately chestnut trees. At the northern end, there was an inlet for a storm drain where the water was warm enough to stay unfrozen in the winter, and exotic ducks and graceful swans swam in endless circles, waiting for a handout. When a toddler, my father managed to fall into one of the shallow lakes as he leaned out of his carriage to feed the ducks, wailing as he sat on the muddy bottom, more wet than in danger.

Oldemor means 'ancient-mother,' and she was both old and old-fashioned. A photograph of her was taken about the time I knew her, when she was in her late eighties. Her fingers are gracefully posed by the side of her face just above her slightly hairy chin. She has a brown splotch on her temple, probably a 'liver spot.' Around her neck are several gold chains and a long string of pearls. She is venerable and beautiful.

Christel Louise Augusta Schultz, born in 1857, was the daughter of Admiral Schultz. I envied her magnificent string of names and regretted that I was just a plain Anne. Far had a sketch of the admiral as a young man, signed J. P. Schultz. Was it a self portrait? He certainly didn't look like an admiral. His handsome face had large deep set eyes and small mouth which he passed down to his grandson and great grandson, my father. The wavy hair he didn't pass on.

"Why couldn't I have inherited some of those lovely curls?" I asked, admiring his picture.

"He probably had it waved at the barber's every morning," Far said.

The answer shocked me. Could such a thing be, a man having his hair curled? They must have used a curling iron like the one Mor heated over the gas burner in the kitchen to fix my hair for parties. At least he didn't have to have a permanent wave every six months as I did. I always hated the heavy curlers, each end of which was plugged into a big machine on wheels. A current passed through the curlers, heating the chemicals and changing my straw hair to fat sausages. The heat burned my scalp, and the hairdresser always seemed irritated when she had to cool my scalp with a jet of cold air. Just imagine the admiral with his hair in big rollers surrounded by gossiping house-wives. Wouldn't that be a sight?

Oldemor was left a widow in 1910, the year before Far was born. Family stories of her strong and spirited personality were told and retold, years after she died soon after the end of the war.

As a young lady at tea in the garden she said, "Quick, give me a cigarette. I want to see the shock on sister Agathe's face when she comes back."

Her older sister, Tante Agathe, embroidered a sampler when she was ten that Mor kept in the linen chest; it was almost a hundred years old. She was a spinster and in her will, left several of her things to my mother, not just as the wife of her favorite great-nephew but because she took a fancy to Mor. There was a beautiful set of pale green English faience dinnerware which we used for many years. I was fascinated by the irregularities in the pattern repeated around the rim. I imagined that someone had stamped the design by hand around the edge of each plate. The design didn't always come out even, so the last one was usually cramped or just a partial repeat. Mor also inherit-ed Tante Agathe's portable sewing machine. It had a fine wooden case and a little hand crank on the side. The bobbin was a tiny metal spool less than an inch long. Mor used it to mend sheets and my dresses, and sometimes I was allowed to sew, too. It worked much better than my little toy machine which always jammed.

Oldemor's eldest daughter was also named Christel, but she died at the age of five. The remaining four sons and youngest daughter Elise (called *Musse*) were brought up strictly, their mother controlling their lives even after they had families of their own. To keep the boys in line she tapped them on the top of the head with her thimble; it was effective but remembered with resentment.

"I used to beat one boy with the other," she told in a loud voice. My literal mind had trouble visualizing this frail ancient lifting my two hundred and fifty pound grandfather. She always spoke loudly because she was hard of hearing; each word carefully pronounced without slurring. She was a lady with perfect diction.

When I was born, she came to the hospital to inspect the new member of the family. "Visiting hours are over," she was told.

Sweeping the nurse aside with her cane, she marched inside declaring, "But *I* am the great-grandmother."

She had an upright piano. Did she ever play? As a well-educated young lady, she must have known how, but I never heard her. During the last year of the war, Far worked at a hospital nearby. He and a couple of friends would sometimes go to her apartment during their lunch hour and relax by playing chamber music.

The telephone rang. "I can not talk to you now," Oldemor shouted into the phone. "I am having a concert."

One morning, about the time the government resigned, the city woke in the middle of the night to loud explosions. The eastern sky was filled with light. Far told me about it and explained, "Uncle Paul ordered the Danish fleet scuttled rather than have it fight on the side of the German navy. He feels very badly. A captain is trained to go down with his ship rather than have it be dishonored by the enemy, and Uncle Paul had to destroy his whole fleet while he was safe on land." Uncle Paul was Oldemor's youngest son. As a commodore in the Navy and chief of the coastal fleet he had been following in his grandfather the admiral's footsteps. At family parties he delighted in telling us about his adventures on the high seas. This latest story, he

Christel Luise Augusta Schultz Ipsen and stern husband, Chief Justice Johannes Ipsen. Daughter Elsie is between her parents, four sons stand in back: Edward, Paul, Christian, and Johannes (my grandfather); their respective wives are: Ellen, Eva, Sophie, and Emma. Baby Christel is my aunt.

did not want to tell. I could barely comprehend what had taken place; these events were too serious for my experience.

Visiting Oldemor meant a trip across town through the parts of the city which were familiar from shopping trips with Mor, and some that I rarely saw. We caught the No. 2 streetcar at the corner near our apartment building. We could always tell which line was coming while it was still far away, because the numeral '2' was painted on large signs on the four curved corners of each bright yellow car. I knelt on the long seat by the window so I could see the sights, and chattered and asked questions as I settled in for the long ride. We stopped at Knippelsbro, one of the large draw bridges spanning the channel separating Christianshavn from the main part of the city. I watched, fascinated as always at the sight of the huge bridge, streetcar tracks and all, rising almost vertically high above our heads.

"Does anyone ever get caught in the middle of the bridge while it's going up?" I wondered, shuddering at the fearful thought. "Would one have time to run to the top as it started to go up and balance there, or maybe grab onto the side railing, until it came back down again? Or would one slide down and fall through the crack and into the channel with a big splash? Maybe if one yelled loudly, the operator in the control tower would stop the bridge from going all the way up."

I spun out the fantasy in my mind as we crossed the now horizontal bridge and continued into town. Along the canal to the left was the outdoor fish market. Boats, trailing water-sloshed floats filled with live fish, were lined up along the dock to sell their wares. To the right, small sailing schooners from the southern coastal farms were moored, filled with their produce. Wednesdays, Mor and I often went to the 'cheese' boat. The handsome, bearded dairy farmer-sailor skimmed off a sliver of cheese, balanced it on the tip of his knife, and stretched up his arm to Mor, standing on the dock above him, so we could sample his wares .

"Too strong," I said, and Mor promised to buy my usual mild 'school-cheese' at Irma's around the corner from where we lived.

The streetcar rumbled by the huge equestrian statue of Bishop Absalon, the warrior cleric who founded Copenhagen in the thirteenth century. "Is that a bird or a plume on top of his helmet?" I wondered, just as the white seagull flew away to dive at a fish in the canal. Absalon, his head and shoulders covered by white droppings, stonily surveyed his realm and ignored the insolent bird.

We swung by the big department store, Magasin du Nord, matched on the other corner by the fashionable Hotel d'Angleterre. "Why does the biggest department store have a French name and so does the fanciest hotel in Denmark, only it's called 'England'?" I asked Far.

"They think it sounds sophisticated," Far said. "When I was a student, Oldemor used to lecture me, 'I do not want to hear that you have been seen eating at d'Angleterre. You can not afford it and you do not have the time.' At that time the terrace of the hotel was *the* fashionable place to meet, but Oldemor didn't approve." Far was very good at mimicking her precise diction and commanding voice. During the war, the hotel was frequented by top-level Germans so I averted my eyes as we went by. Part of 'passive resistance' was to pretend the soldiers did not exist.

Turning the corner by the huge park-like square, *Kongens Nytorv*—King's New Market, we got off in front of the Royal Theater to wait for the No. 10 streetcar.

"Why is the square called 'new' when it's been here hundreds of years?" I asked.

"Because the square at the other end of that street is called the 'Old Market'" was Far's unsatisfying answer.

Why do people do things like that, call something 'new' even though they expect it to still be there ages later. Don't they plan ahead? Why do they want to confuse everyone?

We twisted down Broad Street, which was so narrow that the streetcar barely fit. There was room for one set of tracks, the return route being one block over. Broad Street was very familiar since we bicycled this way to the station to catch the train to the country. I was always scared that my wheels would stick in the streetcar tracks as we crisscrossed them to weave through traffic.

"Here's another confusing name: 'Broad' Street is so narrow it has to be one-way," I said, ever eager to point out the illogical.

"Do you know how it became one-way?" Far asked. "On the day the Germans surprised us with their invasion, I didn't know quite what to do, but thought it best to report for duty at the Military Hospital. You remember, the newsboy told me to take off my uniform? I was bicycling home after being dismissed, and the traffic was a mess, as usual. I was right in back of a small German tank, and we were met head on by the usual jam of bicycles, baby carriages, and pedestrians flooding into the square. I heard the German lieutenant swearing as his tank stalled. '*Das ist doch zum Hollen!*'—this is hell,' he yelled. Two hours later the streets were one-way."

"But they should've left *Strøget* alone," Far added sourly.

Strøget consists of four, old, crooked, connected city streets, running from City Hall to King's New Market. It has been the main shopping district in downtown Copenhagen, forever. As in ancient Rome, the streets are closed to all but pedestrian traffic after ten o'clock in the morning, when the trucks have finished their deliveries. The Germans ordered the streets opened so their tanks and cars could more conveniently cross town between their barracks and headquarters. The Danes were furious at the break in tradition, and some pointedly strolled in the middle of the street, glaring at the invaders' cars.

Our streetcar soon made a sharp left turn onto Silver Street. "I can just see the green copper tops on the towers of Rose Castle," I pointed out, bouncing up and down on the seat. "When I was little, I thought that's where Sleeping Beauty lived." In Danish, she is called *Tornerose*— 'Briar Rose,' so my mistake was natural.

The castle does indeed look like it belongs in a fairy tale. It was designed by my favorite king, the colorful Christian IV. When new it lay outside the city walls. Now, it is a city museum, displaying the crown jewels and other royal treasures, but housing The Royal Guards at one end. Every morning they march across town, around the King's New Market, and on to the palace, for the change of the watch. During the war, however, the national treasures were squirreled away to safety, and German soldiers lived in the fairy castle. As we went past, I saw it there, asleep behind the high wall and locked gates, waiting for a prince to liberate us all.

We continued along Silver Street through Silver Market Square and close to Isaiah's Church. It is an Orthodox Jewish neighborhood, so the place names probably reflect old traditions from the last century when Jews were first allowed to live in Denmark, just outside Copenhagen. During the early years of the war, Danish Jews lived there very quietly, hoping to avoid confrontation with the Germans. After the autumn of 1943, however, the street became deserted; the Jews had all left for asylum in Sweden. Also, after that time, the fish and produce boats no longer came to the old canal because they were forbidden to sail along the coast; too many of the fishermen and farmers had helped the Jews across the water to Sweden from collection points along the shore. Was my handsome Viking from the cheese boat one of the heroes? Was he safe or had he been captured?

Oldemor lived in style in a spacious turn-of-the-century apartment on the far side of *Sortedams Søen*— 'Black Dam Lake.' Her street was wide, paved with cobblestones, and lined with huge horse chestnut trees. It was called Sortedams Dosseringen— 'Black Dam Embankment,' probably because it is on top of the old dam which originally formed the lakes. Two blocks over is a wide avenue called *Blegdamsvej*— 'Bleaching Dam Road,' so named because long ago, the town's women washed linens there and then spread them out on the meadow to be whitened by the sun. Oldemor 'owned' her apartment. I couldn't understand how one could own an apartment; to whom did the roof, stairs, and front door belong?

Having crossed the lake, we got off at the next corner and walked through an old slum district and on to her building overlooking the lake.

"What are those funny little black things that hang outside all the windows?" I asked.

"They're curved mirrors. The old ladies can sit by their windows and see everything that goes on up and down the street. They love to gossip, saying things like, 'There's the Mayor's cat, I wonder where he's going?'" Far quipped.

"Neat! Let's get one for Oldemor so she can look out her window and see us coming."

"She would not like that," he said firmly.

Here was yet another lesson to be stored away about proper manners. Life was full of these rules. One of Mor's was, "Ladies don't smoke on the street." That was from when we had lunch together downtown and she wouldn't leave the restaurant until she'd finished her cigarette, no matter how much I begged to go home. Or, little girls curtsy as they shake hands with adults; not a deep formal sweep to the ground, just a little bob with one knee called a *kniks*. But relatives liked a kiss even if I didn't know them very well. Once Grandmother was insulted when she was in town, and I gave her a kniks and shook her hand when we said good-bye. Oldemor seemed to appreciate good manners and kniksing to her was all right.

In retrospect, visiting Oldemor was a privilege, but at the time it was one of those family occasions where one has to behave no matter how boring it is. She usually sat by the window on a red velvet chair, like a next-generation Victoria, queen of her family. Sometimes she offered hard candy from a little round silver container on the table filled with the knickknacks and family photographs. 'Breast sugar,' she called it— I suppose they were cough drops.

"I wonder if there's candy in the box today. I wonder if she'll remember to offer me some," I thought. One was not supposed to ask. During the latter part of the war, sugar was rationed and I was no longer offered candy but never realized why. Oldemor always used to have 'breast sugar' in the little box.

Her dark blue dress reached to the tops of her high black boots. "I really ought to buy some new boots," she said, stretching her feet in front of her, "but I have had these for thirty years, and they have worn very well."

She had a box of wooden blocks under the table in the living room which I was graciously allowed to play with, when we came to visit. I once said something to Far about them.

"We played with those damned blocks as children, too—and had to put them back when we were done," he laughed.

I liked putting them away because it had to be done just right or they wouldn't fit in the box. How many little hands had lined up those blocks, carefully put them back in their wooden case, and then sliding the cover shut along the little grooves on the sides?

The war confused Oldemor. "I thought the butcher was my friend, but he would not give me enough meat," she complained.

One day the maid threatened to quit and had to be soothed. She had been fined because of 'impertinence.' "But I have always fined them. Help is not what it used to be," Oldemor said, shaking her head.

One day in October, 1943, Far went to visit Oldemor because we had heard that Cousin Clara, also in her eighties, had been sent to concentration camp. She had come to Denmark from the Virgin Islands as the bride of Oldemor's brother who had been there as an officer in the Danish fleet before the islands were sold to the United States in 1919. The two widowed sisters-in-law were good friends. No one thought about it, but Clara was half-Jewish, and the Gestapo had found her name on the list of donors at the Temple. She, her hearing trumpet, and two daughters (in their sixties) had been arrested and sent to a concentration camp with the few hundred other Danish Jews who didn't manage to escape. The family was outraged and complained to the government, the government complained to the Gestapo. Clara was hardly in a conspiracy against Hitler and hardly a danger to the master race. Besides, her two daughters were only a quarter Jewish, and supposedly that was Aryan enough to be acceptable. Finally, the daughters were allowed to come home again. They went to live quietly in the country, afraid to talk to anyone of their experiences for fear of endangering their mother. Clara stayed in Theresienstadt. Rules are rules, and neither logic nor humaneness was a consideration. The commandant did, however, give her special quarters; after all, she was the wife of a naval officer and therefore deserved some special treatment.

She was in charge of a gasoline pump, hearing trumpet and all. "If I hadn't been so mad at those Nazis, I would have died long ago," she said at the end of the war. Like many of the Danes sent to concentration camps, she survived to come home in 1945. About seven thousand Jews escaped from Denmark to Sweden. The Gestapo succeeded in arresting less than five hundred, including Clara. Only about fifty of them died in Theresienstadt; that miracle was accomplished by a king and a people who held the Germans accountable for every Dane, kept lists and persisted.

During the last year of the war, Mor did volunteer work for the Danish Red Cross. I understood that her job was to keep records of Danes in German concentration camps and to organize shipments of food packages to them. I was told they were Danish political prisoners but wasn't too sure what that meant. Mor explained that they were not criminals but soldiers, policemen, and captured members of the Underground. They were in prison camps only because of their resistance to the Germans. The fact that some of the prisoners were Jews was not mentioned; it was not relevant because they were all Danes. None of us realized just how terrible those 'prisons' were.

I didn't come with Far to visit Oldemor that terrible day in October 1943, but have heard the story so many times that I remember it as clearly as if I had. I certainly didn't understand what had happened until much later. Her maid said she was down by the lake. I see her there, sitting on a bench under a big chestnut tree, small and dejected, staring at her boots.

"They have taken Clara to Bohemia," she whispered, as if her sister-in-law had been kidnapped to a wild place beyond civilization. She surely had.

Six

The Red Lamp

When I was about three or four and too young to remember, Mor decided we ought to have a cabin in the country for weekend trips. She saw a red kerosene lamp in a store and brought it home. "I want a house to go with this lamp," she announced. Her imagination was like that. She could see something, construct a whole life around it, and then describe it to us so we too could try the fantasy on for size.

She found a model of a prefab log cabin which had just the right rustic look, and a piece of farm land by Esrum Lake within an easy drive of Copenhagen. The land was bought and the assembly of the house began.

We went up to see the progress, and Far pulled the car off the road onto the field. I jumped out and was shocked to see something other than pavement under my feet, and not even grass like in a park. "Why does it look so funny?" I asked. The farmer who had owned the land had just finished harvesting the wheat, and the stubble looked very strange to a city girl like me.

The cornerstones of the cabin were in place; that was it, no foundation, no walls, no roof, just four cement blocks at the corners of what was to be our cabin. "They did it all wrong. This is much too small!" Mor complained.

We drew lines on the dirt to mark where the walls were going to be and then lay down in the 'bedrooms' to reassure ourselves that there was indeed enough room. Far stretched out his arms and showed me that the distance between the end of his fingers on one hand to the end of the other, was very close to his height. "It's a good trick to know for measuring without a meter stick," he said.

The next time we came to Esrum, *Huset* was finished. We always called it simply 'the house,' not succumbing to the custom of naming it a corny 'Bide-a-Wee.' The half-round logs were stacked and joined by tongue-and-groove joints to form both inner and outer walls. No plaster, just logs and open rafters up to the wooden boards which formed the underside of the roof. When it rained, it was very cozy to curl up with a book and listen to the patter on the roof. The rooftop was supposed to be planted with grass sod for an authentic Norwegian look, but Mor thought grass would bring bugs into the house, so it was just covered with long strips of tar paper. When I was older, I played on our hot tar roof, being very careful to stay at least twenty feet away from the power lines coming into the house at the kitchen end. Grass would have been nicer. I would have liked a sod roof like the one on Uncle Søren's summer house by the coast. It was fun to visit him and sit up there surrounded by wild flowers, like in the middle of a meadow, and look out over the sail boats on the water. I would also have liked a flag pole with a beautiful red-and-white Danish flag, but in the late thirties, before the war, patriotism was not fashionable. My parents had a much more international point of view.

There was a kitchen, a large central living room, and a master bedroom. Off the living room, separated by double glass doors, was a study-guest room. Imagine, they had built bunk beds on one wall of the study, when Mor had told them we wanted one bed on each side of the doors. That problem was quickly fixed. Usually I slept there under the bookshelves on the wall, but sometimes I chose the tiny maid's room off the kitchen. The log walls were unfinished. Gradually cracks formed in the joints between the logs, and we had to stuff felt into the spaces. Far varnished the walls to seal the wood, but it never dried properly; in some places they were permanently sticky, like fly paper.

The logs were stained dark brown on the outside. Mor talked about painting the windows blue and maybe putting screens up to keep the flies out, a novelty that I had never seen. I didn't like the idea. It sounded as though we were to have bars at the windows. How could the windows be opened to let in the sun and air if they were all covered up, and how could I climb in and out? As for blue paint, that was an even worse idea. Wouldn't the house be very dark inside if the windows were blue? Imagine my surprise when they were indeed painted. "Oh, the paint goes *around* not *on* the glass." I thought, but never confessed my confusion to the grownups.

The living room furniture was from my parents' first apartment. The easy chairs, and dining table and chairs were of laminated beech wood. "Anne, never buy blond furniture—one tires of it very quickly," Mor warned me many times. But it was fine for the country, and our city apartment was refurnished in late-1930's fashionable Danish oak. The red lamp hung from the beam over the dinning table at one end of the living room. That is where we ate, Mor and Far played bridge after dinner, and I drew pictures. Their first bed was also brought to the country. It was a double bed, called 'Hollywood' style, really no more than an inner spring mattress on stumpy legs. It soon seemed too small and a second double bed was added even though there was barely room to walk between them. A small built-out closet and a little dressing table provided enough storage for our few summer clothes.

There were two doors into the house, one on the west from the sandy road into the kitchen, and one from the porch on the eastern side into the living room. From the open porch, we had a magnificent view over the lake. The kitchen door was a split 'Dutch door,' so we could open just the top and enjoy the sunset over the pine trees on that side of the house. The tall pines were not a forest, just a small stand of trees, planted on the west side of the field as a wind-break to protect it from erosion. Inside the kitchen there was a little trap door in the floor down to a small cooler for keeping beer and soda. We also had an ice box and usually brought a block of ice in the car when we came up for the weekend.

The amenities were pretty basic. We heated the house on chilly evenings by piling wood in a small Franklin stove in the living room, got water from a hand pump on the north side of the house, cooked on kerosene burners, and of course, lit the living room with the magical red lamp. We had a large metal tub for washing clothes and people. On warm days we filled it in the morning, let it sit in the sun during the day, and then the water was warm enough for a comfortable bath by evening. On cold days we put the tub on the Franklin stove to heat. The kitchen sink drained out into a septic tank by the kitchen door. You could tell the spot by the very lush stand of stinging nettles which grew happily in front of the little combination outhouse and storage shed.

Two red water buckets were kept just inside the kitchen door and carried outside to the pump to be filled. I used to hang from the handle so my weight would bring it down, and pump up the wonderful cold, clear liquid. It took both hands for me to carry the full bucket to the kitchen. The water splashed all over my legs and shoes as it bounced against my knees.

A water dowser had come to look for water—not down by the lake where the neighbors all had wells, but up on top of the hill, convenient to the house. He located a spring and insisted it was there even when everyone was ready to give up. The men dug and re-dug through the loose sandy soil, more suited for potatoes than well holes. He was right; they eventually found water, and installed the pump. Daily, we defied gravity and benefited from the mystical skill of the dowser. Even so, it took a lot of hanging from the handle to raise the water to the top of that hill. One spring, when we pumped our first supply, frightened birds flew out of the spout and a filthy swallow's nest plumped into the bucket. After that, we covered the spout with netting whenever we closed up the house in the fall.

Along the wall of the house beside the door was a long shelf where I brushed my teeth on warm summer evenings, and Mor cooked on the kerosene burners. She called it her 'summer kitchen.' I liked watching Far pump the little piston on the kerosene burners to light them for Mor. They had originally been used on prewar camping trips when my parents hiked in Sweden and drove through Europe on their way to scientific meetings. Dinner was often late because the burners cooked very slowly. As we waited, Far told me of their adventures climbing in the Alps, driving on steep mountain roads, and camping in their little Morris convertible along the roads of Yugoslavia.

We didn't have to suffer the inconvenience of the burners for very long. There was a rural electrification project, and the power company was willing to bring the line down from the main road and into the four or five lake-side cabins, if all the owners became customers. So we installed electric lights and a large electric stove. The stove had four burners and a wonderful oven; it was so big it covered up half the trap door to the cooler in the kitchen floor. The kerosene burners were put in the shed on the shelf with paintbrushes, garden tools, and a bag of rusty nails. I played with the little pump on the burner while sitting on the drafty hole of the outhouse seat. Under the hole was a big metal can whose smelly contents were periodically buried in the garden. The outhouse had started out next to the kitchen door, but was later moved further from the main house, on the other side of the pump. The new location was a little inconvenient in the middle of the night, but during the day one could immodestly leave the door open to enjoy the magnificent view over the lake—and the fresh air. My old training potty from the city was brought up to the house to serve night duty. Men had it easier, especially at night. "I think, I'll go out and admire the stars," Far used to say with a grin, on his way to bed.

One day a professional photographer showed up with a big wooden large-format camera and offered to make picture postcards of the house. He covered his head with a dark cloth and let me see the upside-down image on the ground glass. Some weeks later, the cards arrived: in the background, a guest is just entering the outhouse— what a laugh, caught in the act for eternity.

The coming of electricity was fortuitous as well as convenient, because the war made kerosene—and even candles—difficult to get, so we could no longer light the red lamp. The power lines came directly over the Sound from Sweden, which had an abundance of hydroelectric power. Best of all, there was no rationing of this strange import, as there was in the city where electricity was generated from coal.

The start of war brought other changes. The house had originally been intended for weekend trips, while the rest of Europe was for vacations (at least for my parents). Now travel outside of Denmark was impossible, the car was sold, and I learned to ride my new bike. Going to the country became an "expotition," as Far used to say, quoting Winnie-the-Pooh. We pedaled across the city to the railway station where we put ourselves and the bikes on the train to Humlebœk, on the north coast of the Sound. Then we biked the fifteen kilometers (about nine miles) inland along country highways to the house, the last kilometer struggling along the rutted sandy road

Caught in the act for eternity.

down to the lake. Far carried all our clothes and supplies in a big canvas rucksack. Sometimes my young legs got tired, but Far would put his hand around my forearm and boost me up the hills. Halfway there was a long wonderful coast down a hill with a great country bakery at the bottom. Fresh bread and tomorrow's breakfast rolls were a 'must' addition to the supplies. Then we each had an ice cream cone to give us energy for the rest of the trip.

Once Mor discovered a myriad of white mushrooms on one of the fields along the way. These were the kind it was okay to eat; Mor knew about such things. We picked our way between the grazing sheep and their droppings, filling our bicycle baskets with snowy treasure. The owner came and chased us away. What a grouch! Only later did I understand that we had been stealing his market crop.

Just beyond the mushroom field, the road was lined with beautiful Japanese cherry trees. In the spring, when we went to the house for the Pentecost holidays and came around the turn in the road, we would stand up on our bikes, crane our necks, and ask, "Who can see the cherry trees? Are they in bloom yet?" If we saw pink clouds off in the distance, we knew that the little cherry tree by our house would also be wearing spring colors.

On top of a hill, near the tip of the lake, was a church. It wasn't the typical small Danish country church with whitewashed walls, but a more imposing red brick building with a red tile roof and a bell tower topped by a rooster weather vane. On clear summer evenings and Sunday mornings, we could hear the bells sound faintly over our end of the lake.

Every year, when we sweated up that long hill and saw the weather vane in the distance, I exclaimed, "Look, there's a real stork on top of the tower; this year it's real!" My persistence became a family joke. Storks were a rare treat, a sighting considered good luck.

When the stork inevitably turned into the boringly familiar weather vane, my disappointment was quickly overcome by the sight of the beautiful lake spread below, the long coast down the hill, and the knowledge that we were almost home. Sure enough, soon there was the white-washed old farm house with the thatched roof by 'our' sandy road. We turned and biked the last kilometer down to the lake.

The Japanese cherry tree was planted when we first built the house. Every year I had my picture taken in front of it. At first, it is hard to see whether the tiny stick is holding up the little girl or vice versa. We both grew, the tree following me through the self-conscious giggles and missing front teeth, as it became more and more full, but never very large. In the pictures, it is always about twice my height, with branches spreading out just over my shoulders as if I were a Druid celebrating a spring festival. Except for our strawberry patch, that tree was our most successful planting. Around the house there was an indifferent lawn which Far cut with a hand mower; the rest of the grass grew wild with a profusion of daisies and other flowers. Periodically, Far mowed it with a large farmer's scythe. Scraggly silver poplars and birch trees rimmed the three sides of our land, including the boundary between us and the neighbors to the north. An assortment of apple and pear trees dotted the slope down toward the lake, but had a poor time in the sandy soil and cold winters. Eventually, most died and the rest were stunted, never bearing fruit. There were abortive experiments with asparagus and rhubarb. One summer when tobacco was in very short supply, we even grew that for Far's pipe, but without great success, especially since we had no idea of how to cure the leaves.

We may not have had much of a garden, but we had glorious strawberries. Danish strawberries are special; for three weeks in the early summer they are eaten every day in every possible way. Ours were even better. The patch was on the hillside and the afternoon sun plumped and warmed the huge berries. "They're as sweet as bananas," Mor claimed, but I had forgotten that prewar import.

We also grew garden lettuce and radishes for salads. During our first spring at the house, Mor and I were planting, poking holes in the ground with a garden dibble and dropping in the seeds. "Where do babies come from?" I wanted to know. The metaphor was obvious, but my understanding of the explanation limited.

In a couple of days, I asked, "I've been thinking. How *does* the far get the seed into the mor?"

"Enough was enough. After all, you were only four years old," Mor told me later. That was the end of my sex education for a long time.

In the city, we didn't have a stove but, as in most homes of the time, just a tile table with gas jets mounted on the wall behind it. On top of the table were separate burners connected by little rubber hoses to the gas jets. They were much like the Bunsen burners we later had in chemistry lab, only bigger and with a square grill on top for holding the pots and pans. The oven was also separate, a box that was usually kept on the floor, but lifted onto the table and 'plugged' into the gas when we needed to use it. By contrast, the modern electric stove in the country was a luxury with its large built-in oven.

Mor, normally a good cook, became inspired. She baked large round loaves of fragrant yeasty bread. It was a ritual; without ever measuring she scalded milk and sugar on the stove, cooled it in a flat clay bowl, mixed in the little cake of yeast, and set the milky mixture aside until it bubbled mysteriously. She added scoops of flour and stirred with a wooden spoon. Her silver wedding band came off and was put in the window sill where it wouldn't get lost, and then she plunged her hands into the sticky dough. It was my job to pour small scoops of extra flour onto the wooden counter and then over her hands so she could 'wash' off the stickies. And the fun began. I had my own little piece, pinched off the mother loaf, and Mor and I would squish, knead, and punch the dough until the gluten made it shine. Then it had to rise, covered discretely with a dish towel, sometimes quickly in the sun-warmed bedroom if we were making bread for dinner, sometimes overnight in the cool kitchen. There the temperature was just right for the dough to slowly rise and be ready the next morning, in time to bake breakfast rolls. No matter how many rolls Mor made, we always ate them all while they were still warm, with butter and jam dripping over the edge. Bread lasted a little longer.

As the war progressed and we had more and more shortages, Mor became more and more inventive in the kitchen. Meat was difficult to get in the country because Mor wasn't a 'steady customer' in Esrum. Sometimes we brought a large roast with us from the city, but a large roast, when one has only a family of three, lasts a long time and gets very dry on the third and fourth day. Mor invented a new sauce, a sort of hollandaise cum bernaise sauce, which would have made shoe leather delectable. Because of rationing, she used just a little butter and the whole egg, then added onions, parsley, and milk to make a marvelous concoction. It could only be made on the even-heating burners of the new electric stove. Anywhere else or in anyone else's hands, the sauce invariably curdled.

Frankfurters, called 'Danish sausages,' inspired another recipe, still a family favorite. The hot dogs were cut on the diagonal (the oval shape of the slices is a *sine quo non* of the recipe); browned with onions and cubes of potato; sauced with milk, ketchup, vinegar; thickened with a little flour; and flavored with parsley. My job was to chop the parsley on the wooden cutting board. I rocked the big curved 'French knife' back and forth on the little mound of green leaves for a long time. "Not fine enough; do it some more," Mor always said.

The undependability of the meat supply lead to a family saga. One weekend we were expecting company at the house. Mor, who didn't want to risk her reputation as a hostess, telephoned the butcher in the city and ordered a roast to be sent by train that afternoon. Usually this was a reliable method of delivery, but there was a mix-up and a heat wave, and the roast did not arrive on the expected train. Several days later, the postman came on his bike bringing a notice of delivery from the wrong station and an insistence on personal pickup. Far and guest had to go to a different town to claim it. The baggage handler firmly requested that they immediately remove the very malodorous package crawling with flies and maggots and explained that, since it had been mailed by the Royal Post, he, as baggage handler, was not allowed to dispose of it. After his visit, the guest mailed us a scroll of toilet paper in place of the usual bread-and-butter letter. On it, he had written a long poem, a ballad of the ill-fated roast, to be sung to a familiar tune. I marveled that anyone could be so creative and *funny*.

When we first built the house, peddlers' wagons with groceries, milk, or meat would come right to our door, each on their appointed days of the week. Or we would simply drive to the nearest town for ice and food. When the war started, all these conveniences vanished. Then we got milk every day from the little farm on the sandy road by the highway. There were two boys in the family who delivered the milk, still warm from the cows. We pasteurized it by heating it in a big pot on the stove, but usually it boiled over to repeated jokes about watched pots and spilt milk. In the morning we could spoon off a layer of cream, as thick as butter—marvelous on the strawberries from the garden. Thick cream was a luxury, unknown by then in the city.

When Mor heard that the farmer had tuberculosis, we stopped getting his milk, even though the cows were checked and certified tuberculosis-free. We then started picking it up at the modern dairy farm a little further down the road. They had milking machines, and I watched, fascinated by the sight of the white fluid running along the glass tubes and emptying into the waiting milk cans. We poured some into our pail; then the big cans were covered and rolled out to the edge of the main road for pickup by the dairy co-op's wagon.

Esrum Lake is especially beautiful. It is a large oval and lies about thirty miles north of Copenhagen. The water is miraculously clear and the fishing legendary. The surrounding countryside has rolling hills of sandy soil, good for growing potatoes. I don't know much about geology, but our end of the lake looks like the bottom was suddenly lowered by about twenty-five feet. Walking down the hill from the house toward the lake for about a hundred feet, one suddenly comes to the edge. The steep slope is covered with tall trees whose tops can barely be seen from the house. Far built a path down the slope with hairpin turns and log steps supported by pegs. The lake shore was only a narrow strip of land shaded by the tall trees and separated from the lake by man-high reeds. They were the kind of reeds used to thatch the old farm by the main road. One summer I made a hula skirt by stringing the long skinny leaves on a ribbon tied around my waist. A passage was cut through the reeds to the open water where it was deep enough to swim. Two planks formed a narrow dock and then was widened to accommodate a couple of deck chairs.

Along the southern end of the lake lies a large ancient forest of Danish oak and beech. We used to sit on the porch and enjoy the spring green of the beeches and the fall russets of the oak. It was also a wonderful, safe place to watch the lightning over the trees. I would have been frightened of the thunderstorms, but Far convinced me that the water of the lake and the large trees of the forest drew the lightening away from us. At each flash of light, we counted the seconds until the thunder came.

One hot summer afternoon, I pointed to the forest and asked, "Far, what's that strange black cloud?"

"What do you know, that's a tornado," he answered. "They're big powerful tropical storms that pull up trees by the roots and knock over houses. But we never have tornadoes in Denmark, so I guess it isn't really there."

Esrum is also the name of an old, old town by the west end of the lake. It was probably founded by Vikings using the lake as a safe haven, or maybe it is even older. The medieval Esrum Monastery is still there, now an orphanage, I think. It broods behind a tall wall and iron gate. Far read out loud from a historical novel by Ingemann about the daring deeds of knights and kings in the twelfth century: "...and he spent the night at the monastery in Esrum." Just imagine, the king's best knight stayed at *my* monastery.

Esrumgaard, a large farm between our house and the town, was probably originally the home farm of the monastery, now privately owned. The fields extended down to the lake south of us. A scraggly hedge divided the property from the fields south of our house. They were sort of neighbors, except that we could only see the buildings when we went along the road to the town. The contrast was obvious between the small subsistence farm of about thirty to forty acres where we bought our milk, and the large manor house, extensive barns, and huge fields on the rolling hills.

One day in August we were bicycling to Esrum to buy groceries. As we passed Esrumgaard, we looked across the road to a scene from the turn of the century: a Danish Breughel, an anachronism never to be seen again. That week I had watched in fascination when they reaped the wheat on the small field next to our house. Because of the war, they were using an old harvester pulled by a horse. Rotating arms, like the wings of a mill, bent the grain into the machine, which bound it in bundles and spewed them out to one side. I was allowed to help by gathering lose stalks, tying them in not-so-neat sheaves, and piling everything into large stacks.

Harvesting at Esrumgaard was of a different magnitude. A half-dozen harvesters were windmilling their way up the hillside of unending grain in a wide staggered path, each pulled by several horses. By the edge of the field where the harvesters couldn't go, was a line of men swinging large scythes rhythmically back and forth.

The house was a few miles north of the town. The mail address, when the mailman found his way down our sandy road, was *Esrum per Plejelt*. Plejlt was a tiny village, almost as far from the house as Esrum, but in the other direction along the highway and on top of a steep hill. It consisted of only a few farm houses, clustered by a fork in the road. I remember it, aside from our quaint address, because the sheriff lived there. He was not a mean, villainous, powerful Sheriff-of-Nottingham, but a friendly, Danish farmer-sheriff. I liked to imagine him chasing Robin Hood in our own forest of Gribsskov. We had bought our land from him, and he still owned the fields to the south of us, all the way to the Esrumgaard hedge.

One spring I trudged behind him for an entire day while he steered the horse-drawn plow, preparing the land for planting potatoes, and listened patiently to my chatter. When they were ready for harvest, he told us to please take as many potatoes as we wanted; he couldn't hire help to pick what the mechanical picker left behind. New Danish potatoes, little tiny ones carefully scraped and boiled, are a delicacy. Fresh from the soil, they are even better. Late in the afternoon we would bring a little bucket and shovel down to the edge of the field, and like biblical widows and orphans glean leftover potatoes.

The house next to us on the north side was owned by a time-share cooperative. A group of families owned the cabin together, each having the right to vacation there a week or two. I always hoped that the next weekend would bring children. Sometimes a brother and sister, about my age, would come with their parents. We would then roam around together, swim, play monopoly and tiddlywinks on rainy days, or do whatever kids of that age do. I was impressed when the boy casually relieved himself on the side of a tree, but less impressed with his pale little worm—not to be compared with my handsome father who often worked down by the lake with nothing on but his wooden clogs. The rest of the time, I was mostly alone during the day. I probably drove Mor crazy with my "what can I do?" but I don't remember being bored. Far built a swing, sinking tall wooden posts into the ground. Thick rope and a wooden seat suspended from the joining beam completed this most excellent stimulus of the imagination. I spent hours there, pumping higher and higher until I could see over the roof of the house and steer the plane through the white clouds up to the blue sky. Or I would lie on my stomach and push the seat around and around, twisting the rope so tight that I could barely fit on the seat, and then let go and twirl until the world disappeared in a blur.

Next to the swing was my sandbox. Or was it really an ephemeral garden, with its paths bordered by Johnny-jump-ups and daisies, droopy by supper time? "If you always sit with your back to the sun, you'll still be pale in the face by fall and no one will believe we've been up here all summer," Mor fussed.

One birthday, I received a child-size botanist sample box. It was a little metal cylinder with a lid that hinged open and a shoulder strap. I imagined I was a British botanist collecting rare specimens in Africa like in the photos in the hundred-year-old book in our bookcase. I roamed over the fields to find wild flowers: forget-me-nots by a hidden stream, tiny scarlet pimpernels among the wheat, stork-beak, wild snapdragons with their little fish mouths, bigger daisies, blue bachelor buttons, gorgeous poppies, and red grasses growing next to the lark's nest. "Pick them with long stems," Mor yelled after me as I set out, but she gave me a little egg cup for the tiny bouquet I brought her.

I swam in the lake. Mor complained the water was too cold and seldom went in. It was a proud day when I learned to stay afloat long enough to take a few strokes. I drew a picture. "Anne is swimming, but Mor is afraid of the water," said the caption.

We rowed up and down by the shore of the lake, marveling that we could see through the very clear water all the way to the bottom where the eels slithered across the sand. We found a small patch of blue clay in the shallow water of a little bay. It had to be kneaded to work out the bits of dirt and sand, but then provided hours of creative activity as I produced endless ashtrays and crumbly little animal figures. "Look at my duck," I said. "It's asleep with its beak under one wing." My pride and imagination were greater than my talent. No one else could see what, to me, was so obviously a duck.

Most evenings we had a fire. Far read out loud while Mor warmed herself by the stove, and I curled up, sucking the first two finger of my hand. He read *Winnie-the-Pooh*, *Wind in the Willows*, and later, *Ivanhoe*, *Robin Hood*, *The Last of the Mohicans*, *King Solomon's Mines*, and *Tom Sawyer*. There were also Danish historical novels: *Gyngehøvdingen*, and the series about medieval kings by Ingemann, the Danish Sir Walter Scott. Far read all his favorite childhood adventure stories to me, but never said they were too old for me or only for boys. He made them live by giving each character a different dramatic voice. Once I had heard them read out loud, I could read them by myself, over and over.

Our first trip of the year was usually during the week of Easter vacation. One year, Easter was early. That must have been the year of the long, cold and dreary winter. It seemed to go on forever. Every day when Far came home from work, I demanded, "How cold was it today?"

"Minus twenty—again."

"Is that on the Celsius or Remur scale?" I usually asked.

"Celsius." That was colder.

Weather reports were not allowed on the radio, but Far had shown me the big mercury thermometer at the Institute. It had both the Celsius (centigrade) and the old-fashioned Remur scale that no one used anymore.

Up at the house, the snow was still several feet deep. I built a snow fort by the kitchen door, mixing snow and water for mortar. At bedtime, I crawled into my sleeping bag with all my clothes on. Far slept in a chair next to the little stove so he could get up several times during the night to put more wood on the fire. The wind howled, but the temperature rose and the ice in the lake broke up with loud thunderous crashes that I never heard in my deep sleep.

The next morning, I dressed inside my sleeping bag. "I'm wearing fewer clothes now than last night." I said, laughing.

The rising temperatures had broken the ice into tiny chips which the wind had driven to our side of the lake, pushing them into a huge pile. My fort was solid ice. The sun rose over the lake, reflecting on the bright snow which soon melted. The birds began to sing and the crows flew over the house proclaiming that spring had arrived. The lark spiraled toward the sky, singing loudly that soon the nightingale, the stork, and the cuckoo would return from their winter homes in Egypt.

Although the war was evident everywhere in the city, Esrum was isolated. Nevertheless, the war occasionally intruded, sometimes in scary ways that were stark reminders of reality, but often turning out to be more amusing than dangerous.

One summer morning, Far had left very early to commute to the city. Mor was still in bed, and I went out on the porch to enjoy the view of the lake. I rushed into the bedroom in a panic, "Mor, Mor, there are two German officers on the terrace!"

Mor took a little notebook and a pencil and went outside. She knew how to handle these intruders, by taking advantage of their respect for authority. "Get off my land," she said in German. "This is private property. I want your name, rank, and the name of your commanding officer in order to lodge a complaint." Although she usually pretended not to understand German, and in later years absolutely refused to speak it, she could in fact be quite fluent.

The officers grumbled something but walked around to the other side of the house by the road. I peeked out the kitchen window to see where they went.

"Mor, Mor, there's a whole troop of German soldiers up by the wood."

Just then we heard riffle shots. It was probably merely a signal that the rest stop was over and time for the troop to move on, but we were absolutely convinced that they were going to line us up against the house and shoot us right there. Shaking, Mor grabbed my arm and dashed through the neighbors' yards to the house of our friend, Miss Pongseng. There we collapsed for the rest of the day, repeating our dramatic tale over and over until Far came home, and we could tell of our narrow escape again. We wondered if the Germans were just on a hike, or whether they were looking for evidence of drop sites used by the British to parachute supplies to the Underground.

Once, Ulla came to visit. This was a rare event because she was considered delicate and her parents were very protective. Usually she spent the whole summer on her grandfather's farm far away, but this week she came to visit, a nice surprise. We decided to pick wild cherries. There were some large trees on the Esrumgaard boundary. Two German soldiers suddenly came out of the tall wheat pulling their bicycles. They spoke to us, and when that didn't get a response, started gesturing with their hands. I was too scared to try to understand. Ulla was three years older and was taking German in school but she, too, shook her head and looked baffled. We had strict instructions never to talk to strange men, certainly not to German soldiers. They must have thought we were a couple of really stupid farm girls. After they left, Ulla said they were lost and had asked for the way to the main road.

The brick chimney had originally been painted bright yellow. This is a yellow ocher color often added to lime as a variant of the usual whitewash used on most Danish farm houses. Mor hated it. "I want it *white*," she insisted.

A man came to repaint and also do some repair work on the chimney; it smoked so badly, it's a wonder we hadn't been poisoned by carbon monoxide. He spent the whole day at the relatively simple job, enjoying the view, warm sun, and cool beer. He had such a great time that he refused to be paid at the end of the day, but he asked a favor. He owned a small cabin cruiser and a rowboat, and loved to fish. Since the escape of the Jews, he explained, the Germans no longer allowed boats to be moored along the Sound, to prevent the Underground from using them for illegal trips to Sweden. Our intrepid chimney-fixer-and-fisherman had probably made a few detours himself. Anyway, he wondered if he could use our dock. Since we had a dock and no boat, and he had boats but no dock and only needed them for early morning fishing trips, the arrangement seemed excellent all around. We couldn't use the cruiser for lack of fuel, but the rowboat was ours during the day. Some mornings we would find donations of pike or home-smoked eels by the kitchen door. Whether Far realized it immediately, or it dawned on him somewhat later, it soon became obvious that the very early fishing trips were a blind for Underground pickup of explosive supplies, parachuted from Allied planes in the middle of the night.

One midnight there was an aerial battle between Allied planes and German and Swedish anti-aircraft. When I heard about it the next morning, I complained, "Why didn't you wake me up?

"Don't be silly," Mor said. "If that noise didn't wake you, nothing could."

Admiring a pike, a dawn present from our 'fisherman' friend. On the left is Fru Holm-Johansen my piano teacher.

But I was puzzled by the rules of war and asked, "Why would the Swedes shoot at our side? I thought they were good guys."

"The Swedes have to at least pretend to be neutral. Their shots were even further from hitting anything than those of the Germans, but they set up a wall of anti-aircraft fire that said, 'don't come any further, this is neutral Sweden.' It was quite a fireworks show."

I collected the little foil strips on our field, thinking we could save them for tinsel on our Christmas tree; they had been scattered from the Allied planes to baffle the German search lights.

That day, my parents hovered over the radio listening to the English and Swedish news broadcast. Far had transported the little radio up to the house in his knapsack with the other supplies; a bag of precious rationed sugar had leaked so that ever after the radio smelled of burnt caramel whenever we turned it on. We had brought it partly so we could hear the news in the country, and also to stash it away, a spare in case radios were impounded in the city, as they had been in Norway and Holland. The Germans had installed big static generators in Copenhagen to jam broadcasts from abroad, but in Esrum we were far enough away, so the signal was almost clear.

The three-way air battle that had woken everyone but me was the Allied bombing raid on the big V-2 rocket-bomb production facility at Peenemünde. These were the infamous 'Doodle-bombs' that were devastating London, so named with typical British humor and bravado for their noisy propellant system which warned of their approach. The huge underground assembly site was just southeast of us on the northern coast of German, less than a hundred and fifty miles away. The distance to war was not far, as-the-plane-flies, but a world away from our sanctuary under the magical red lamp.

SEVEN

A Broken Doll, Rabbit Fur, and Science

Mor was my feminine and feminist role model for daily living and relating to people. She was the pragmatist and the survivor, yet the smallest incident could stimulate her imagination. Reading was her escape and also her source of coping with that difficult time. Far was the romantic, the singer of songs, the literary scholar, the amateur musician, and yet the dedicated physician and scientist. I inherited and learned from both of them, from others in the family, and from their friends. Because I was an only child and our lives were constrained by the war, I saw these adults at closer hand than might otherwise have been. I never recognized contradictions among their many role models, but assumed that one could and should do and have it all. To look back and search for the origins of my eventual fascination with science is like trying to trace particular threads in that tapestry of my early childhood; they are inextricably woven among all the other images of people and the everyday. Nevertheless, some incidents and people stand out with particular clarity.

I had always known that Far was a physician. Before I was born, he wrote a lullaby for Mor with a very simple melody so that she would be able to sing it to their expected child. The words tell of a mother's love and a father who is "out where the sick live." It is the only song that I remember her ever singing.

There had never been any question in my father's family but that Far would follow in my grandfather's footsteps and study medicine. Music and literature were taken for granted as a part of the life of a cultured person, but to be a doctor was to serve humanity. Other sciences were also interesting, but only for diversion unless they were useful. My grandfather was a talented amateur artist who filled his house with his watercolors and dedicated many hours to collecting, cataloging, and drawing botanical and zoological specimens. He loved his six children and they adored him in turn, but first of all, he was a surgeon. When he retired he left it all behind, free to pursue his avocations.

"I found a fascinating book on comparative languages," Far enthused one day as a youngster.

"You think that's interesting; here's an even better book on comparative physiology," retorted his equally enthusiastic father.

They also shared their name: Johannes Ipsen, like grandfather's father, as well. Only the two of them were still alive, so to keep them distinct, Far had 'Jr.' after his name.

"It really should be Johannes Ipsen, the third," Mor, the social snob, bragged to me. 'Johannes' is the equivalent of the English 'John,' and since it is such a common name, it is usually abbreviated 'Johs.' It appeared in the family at a time when Germanic names were more fashionable than the common Danish form, 'Jens.' Mor always called him 'Ips.'

Far kept two notebooks as a teenager. He filled them with detailed observations of the life histories of butterflies, from their dietary requirements as caterpillars, through their pupae stage, and to their final magical transformation to butterflies and moths. Nature was grandfather's love and he enthusiastically supported such scientific hobbies, but not as a profession.

Far left the rural town of his teen-age years when he was graduated from gymnasium (high school) and went to Copenhagen to study medicine at Denmark's only university. He was slightly younger than the typical nineteen and emotionally ill-prepared for the sudden freedom of student life away from his family. He drifted through his first year, wooing all the girls with his guitar playing and folk singing, and earned extra money by tutoring so he could buy a kayak.

Once he asked his father about sex. "Just find a girl to love and marry her. Then all your problems will be over," was his unhelpful advice.

"What was I to do when I fell in love with every pretty girl I met?" Far puzzled.

He was rudely awakened at the end of the first year of university when he failed the exam. That first year of study was a general liberal arts program, the *filosofikum*. The final exam was used as a screen for further specialization, such as medicine, and the majority of students failed. Far, however, was so furious with himself that he resolved not to lose a year and studied for his successful retake of the exam while attending the second year lectures. His race to the eventual finish was so successful that he graduated at a very young twenty-three, nearly the same age as his father before him. Mor used to brag that the two of them were the youngest ever to get medical degrees at Copenhagen, but she may have exaggerated.

Far and Mor met while he was still at university. One of Far's favorite activities was to bicycle up to Furesøen, a beautiful lake where someone had donated land for the students to use. Some architecture students had designed a cabin, and a group of them had built it for a cooperative weekend retreat. Far was engaged to another medical student and they were at *Hytten*— 'The Hut' together. Mor had recently left her home in a small town and moved to Copenhagen. One of her friends had invited her to come along to *Hytten*.

It was love at first sight. Mor often told how the two of them bicycled back to the city together after a wild weekend and finished the story with, "We were so tipsy on champagne that we had to rest in a ditch by the road." The rest was censored with a dreamy smile.

Soon Mor's name changed from Frøken Kamma Gerda Ølgaard Rasmussen to Fru Johannes Ipsen, but among friends she was 'Daphne.' She had never liked any of her names: the first was strange (I have never met anyone called 'Kamma'); the second, low class (it was very common); and the last was her father's, and she wasn't speaking to him. She blamed her mother's recent suicide on his drunkenness and inability to keep a job. After her mother died, Mor left home and refused to speak to any of her relatives, except her mother's sister, Moster Rigmor. For a while she used her mother's maiden name, but since 'Ølgaard' literally means 'Beer Inn' that wasn't very classy either. It was, however, responsible for her nickname; one of her artist friends knew a song about an innkeeper named Ølgaard with a daughter called Daphne. Thereafter, Mor's legal names were only used on official documents.

Far's degree from medical school, as was usual, gave him a license to practice as a physician and have the title '*læge*' added to the end of his name; however, a year as an intern was required. Internships to all the hospitals in Denmark were awarded by lottery in which the candidates drew a number and then made their choices in order. The five prestigious hospitals in Copenhagen were, of course, considered the top prizes. Far couldn't get to the lottery, so Mor was dispatched with crossed fingers and a list of choices. With her usual incredible luck, she drew the number five, and Far was therefore assured a place in Copenhagen.

He reported for work on the first day at Bispebjerg Hospital. The head nurse took one look at his boyish good looks and dismissively told him, "Wait over there with the rest of the students."

"I never felt as young and inexperienced as the first night when I was on duty by myself," he often confessed.

He also liked to tell of his first house-call. The youngest doctors were given the night calls for what was already in the mid 1930's the beginning of universal health care in Denmark. The telephone rang. "My niece is visiting from the country and the baby is coming. Please hurry, Doctor," the flustered aunt said but hung up giving neither name nor address.

Twenty minutes later the agitated woman called back, and when reminded that the Doctor needed her address she exclaimed impatiently, "But we've lived here for twenty-five years!"

Far would go on to tell how the experienced midwife could usually be relied on to arrive first and guide the novice doctor through a delivery, but that evening she was not yet there. The baby was presenting awkwardly. "I was so flustered, I couldn't remember anything and nearly panicked. Then reflex took over, and my hands pushed and turned the baby as we had practiced in class. The midwife finally came, just in time to clean up."

By the time of the surprise German invasion of Denmark, Far was completing his compulsory military service in the reserves of the

Medical Corps. "I was in the cavalry," he said with pride and then added with an ironic chuckle, "That meant I got to ride in the sidecar of a motorcycle."

At the same time, he had left general practice to work in the Department of Standardization at the Serum Institute. Far eventually became the head of the section which did the standardization of vaccines and sera for the League of Nations. Some of these activities continued during part of the war, but even when the samples from around the world slowed to a trickle, Far continued his research on vaccines.

He often told Mor and me the following story about the first day of his new job, when he was reporting to the chief of the lab. This man was full of his own importance and was later institutionalized for megalomania.

The pompous new boss showed him around and said, "We have a system of bells here. When you hear two rings, that's your signal to report to my office."

Far thought a minute and then, using a thick rural dialect, told the following parable which he had learned from his father:

> A farmer had hired a new hand. He was showing him around the fields and said, "A ain't a man o' many words. If you're plowin' da field and A's standin' by da house and A goes like dis," he beckoned with his hand and added, "It means you shu'd come."
>
> "A ain't a man o' many words either," said the new helper. "If A's plowin' da field and you're standing by da house and you go like so," he also beckoned with his hand. "And A goes like dis," he shook his head and concluded, "It means A won't come."

The chief of the lab never mentioned the bells again. He may have been crazy but he wasn't stupid. "A ain't a man o' many words" became a family catch phrase for nonconformity. None of us liked to be bossed around.

Dr. Johannes Ipsen as a young father and as a clowning but intrepid scientist, 'shooting' at the photographer with a syringe.

I had only a dim understanding of Far's research. Today he would be called an immunologist, but from my point of view, he played with mice in cages, or shaved the fur off the backs of rabbits and painted checkerboards on their skin. At home during the evening, he wrote neat columns of numbers in ink and made long calculations using his slide rule. The slide rule had a big ink stain over one end of it, obscuring some of the numbers. It was always in his briefcase, handy to use as a ruler when I needed one. If I had been told that I would later spend several college summers in his lab injecting mice and rabbit backs to do bioassays for tetanus and diphtheria anti-toxin, and long hours inverting large matrices on a calculator or drawing graphs in India ink, I would hardly have been surprised; that was what grown-up scientists and doctors did, and I assumed I would be one, too.

When adults asked, "What do you want to be when you grow up?" I always answered, "A doctor."

The adult usually said, "Isn't that nice, just like your father."

Whether because I was an only child, deaf to discouragement, or obviously so determined as to preclude argument, I never got the impression that there was anything unusual about a girl having these plans. Danish society was ahead of most of the world in its feminist thinking, and similar to where the United States is now. In my family, not only were the men professionals: judges and admirals as well as doctors, but Grandmother had been my grandfather's chief nurse before their marriage, and she obviously could run a department with the same firmness as she ran her large household. Of my four aunts, one was a nurse; one a pharmacist who, with her husband, ran the pharmacy that had been in his family for several hundred years; and one was a medical secretary, married to a doctor. Only my youngest aunt stayed at home, although she eventually became a pharmacist. Far always claimed that his eldest sister, Christel, should have been a doctor, but that would have been going a little too far when she was young, my grandfather would not have approved. In my generation, the assumption was that women as well as men would and could be whatever we wanted.

My curiosity was encouraged. Far always took my questions seriously and always seemed to know everything.

One evening in the country, he and I went to fetch the milk. Walking along the one-kilometer sandy road from our cabin to the farm was beautiful in the evening but a fair trek for my young legs. The road angled around two sides of a large field. Far had explained that Danish farmers practice crop rotation, alternating between wheat, rye, oats, potatoes, and grass for the cows. The fields were not fenced, so when it was a grass year, the cows were staked to the ground. They grazed their way around in a circle on their lead ropes, then lay chewing their cud until they were moved to the next part of the field.

It was a grass year. "Let's cut across the field, it's shorter," said Far.

I hesitated. It takes nerve for a little girl to walk across a field with cows, even when Daddy is along. Not only were cows very large and had formidable horns, but they had the disconcerting habit of turning to stare as they thoughtfully chewed their cud. What were they thinking? Maybe, that it would be fun to chase little girls across the field. Those ropes and stakes looked very flimsy.

On this lovely summer evening, the cows were in the barn being milked and the field was safe, but I still didn't think it was a good idea. "It can't be shorter. *I know*," I insisted

"Oh yes, it *is* shorter; the diagonal in a square is like the hypotenuse of a triangle, and the hypotenuse is always shorter than the two sides," my scientist Far eagerly explained about diagonals and hypotenuses.

"But when I was four and we moved from Stormøllevej to Ved Volden, Mor told me to pack my toys, and my shovel wouldn't fit in the box unless I put it on the diagonal, so the diagonal is longer than the side," I insisted, the sentence coming out as if it were all one word.

Far barely hesitated as he digested my breathless explanation, and said, "Longer than *one* side, but we have to walk along *two* sides of the field."

"Ooooh!"

Fascinating! The next day I spent all afternoon drawing little pictures of squares and diagonals on scraps of paper, using Far's slide rule as a straight edge. "What *are* you doing?" he wanted to know.

"I'm trying to see how *much* shorter the diagonal is than the sides." Even then I was an empiricist and liked geometry. The trouble was that I was in second grade and only understood addition and subtraction. I thought I could show that there was a constant difference between the two lengths. My method seemed to give about right answers, but then my squares were all about the same size, and I didn't realize that would make a difference. Learning about the Pythagorean theorem, incommensurability, and irrational numbers were in the distant future. I don't remember Far's response. Wisely, he probably left me to my diagrams; the explanation of my difficulty would have been beyond me anyway.

To be respected in the research community, it was necessary to obtain a degree beyond that needed to be a clinician. A degree of *doktor medicinae*, shortened as 'Dr. med.' requires a research thesis and is roughly equivalent to a Doctor of Science degree in the United States.

Far started his research on the hemolysis of red blood cells. Even before the war he had been interested in quantitative methods applied to medical sciences, and had visited David Finney in England. Finney later wrote the classic work on bioassay, a statistical text which I reverently studied in graduate school. In order to analyze the data, Far studied new statistical techniques with Georg Rasch, a well-known Danish statistician, also associated with the Serum Institute.

Finally the research itself was finished, but the writing went slowly. Mor became impatient and insisted Far go up to our cabin in the country, "— and for heaven's sake, don't come back until it's finished," she ordered.

She loved to tell the story, "I went up to the house with him with a supply of canned food. Ips is so absent-minded that I was afraid he would eat all the food at once, so I put the cans on the kitchen counter and labeled them: Monday, Tuesday, and so on."

By October 1941, the thesis was finished, bound (like a *real* book, I liked to point out), and ready for the defense. This was a very formal affair, open to the public, and had all the trappings of a formal debate. I was invited to come, but thought it sounded very boring. "No, thanks," I said, but eagerly heard about the details afterwards. Each reader, called an 'opponent,' read his prepared critique standing at a podium and was supposed to ask penetrating questions of the candidate who stood at another podium. Instead, Dr. Madsen, the Institute Director and Far's mentor, made a glowing speech about the value of Far's work to science and Denmark's international reputation. Then, also by tradition, the other reader made sure that every 'i' had been dotted and every 't' crossed, while the nervous candidate paged wildly through his copy to find each page in question.

There was also usually an opponent from the audience, only in this case it was Dr. Rasch, Far's colleague and teacher. He began by saying affirmatively, "Dear candidate, let me first of all say, you have written a good book." Then he went on to critique some of the finer mathematical points.

Far passed with flying colors. A glowing report appeared in the next editions of *Politiken* and *Berlingske Tidene*, accompanied by a picture of the candidate, again according to tradition. The news reporters quoted Madsen's remarks at length, and added that Dr. Rasch's comments were so learned that no one understood a word.

From then on Far's letters were addressed to 'Hr. Dr. med. Johs. Ipsen, Jr., Læge' to indicate that he was the son of a man with the same name and had a doctoral degree as well as being a physician. Mor, with the privilege conferred by marriage, was: 'Fru Dr. med. Johs. Ipsen, Jr.' If she too had been a doctor, that title would have been both before and after the 'Fru.'

There was a formal and grand dinner party to celebrate. The ladies wore long dresses and the gentlemen white tie and tails. Mor had on her beautiful gown and Far looked splendid. Despite my six-and-a-half years, I was allowed to come. I was very proud in my first long dress of pale blue brocade and with short puffed sleeves, especially made for the occasion. As the fifty guests arrived, each gentleman took a small card with his name on the front from a tray by the entrance. Inside was written the name of his *borddame*— 'table-lady' whom he was to escort to the dinner table. At Danish dinner parties, an empty tray signaled that all the guests had arrived and dinner could be served. There was a long wait until Mor discovered that, as usual, Far had forgotten to pick up his card. We all had a good laugh at the absent-minded 'doctor' as we went in to dinner, each lady's hand on the right arm of her escort. I too was conducted by a gentleman, a very good friend of Far's, who seemed not at all put out at having to entertain a child.

There had been endless discussions at home on how to arrange the seating so that all conventions of precedence would be met.

Finally, they had found a solution: my grandparents and Dr. and Mrs. Madsen would grace the ends of the long table and my parents could smile at each other across the flowers and candles from the middle of the table. Thus the honors of seniority were reserved for the traditional ends, and the younger crowd could have fun in the middle. There were many courses served by a crew of well-trained waiters, and each was accompanied by a different wine served in its own type of glass. There were several clever speeches, including one by Grandfather, who was a master of the art. As the company mellowed, there were many toasts, public and private. By tradition, a lady was not supposed to drink except during a toast, so it was the duty of each escort and husband to ensure that their ladies had ample opportunity to taste the many wines. Mor told me that in the old days, a wife had the right to demand a penalty of a dozen leather gloves if she felt her husband had neglected her in favor of his 'table-lady' by not giving her sufficient opportunity to drink. I was allowed to restrict myself to plain water.

While the wine and food flowed, song sheets were distributed, especially written for the occasion by various guests and sung by everyone to familiar tunes. One really clever song was sung twice. The first time, we were instructed to use all of the words on a line, and the song appeared to praise Hitler and our German masters. However the second time through, when only part of each line was sung according to the meter of another tune, the song became a satire, blasting the occupation. I thought this was the funniest song I had ever heard, but was half-afraid that someone would report our illegal activities to the Gestapo and we would be arrested. Or worse.

The essence of science is international and non-military, but Far discouraged personal letters from his Italian and German colleagues; even innocent contact with former friends from those countries now aligned with Germany, could be misconstrued by nationalistic Danes. One Italian friend, to show that he understood, sent a large box of luxury foods immediately after Denmark was occupied, to help our presumed hardships. The box was so slow in transit that when it finally arrived, the contents were nearly inedible. We laughed as we cracked our teeth on the rock-hard biscottis and amarettos, but regretted that we could not acknowledge the kind gesture. Although the war cut off most of Far's correspondence and visits with research colleagues around the world, he continued to receive a few letters from the neutral countries such as Sweden and particularly Switzerland. I filled an album with the stamps from Far's exotic international correspondence. I treasured those from Geneva with their special 'League of Nations' postmark and thought that *buying* a stamp from a dealer was cheating.

During the fall of 1942, Far became interested in developing an improved typhus fever vaccine. Typhus fever, like the black plague, is harbored by rodents and spread by lice. These diseases are the devastating companions of war. Far had to get a laboratory strain of typhus on which to test his methods and therefore wrote to his colleague, Dr. Prigge, in Frankfurt-am-Mein, Germany. Arrangements were made, and Far received a travel permit to Frankfurt to pick up the infected mice in person.

"While you're down in Germany, can you please get a new head for the doll Dr. Prigge gave me?" I asked. One day I had sat the beautiful doll on the floor; she had fallen over and broken the back of her delicate porcelain head. I had been very upset that because of war shortages, she couldn't be fixed. I now naturally assumed that since she was from Germany, Far would easily be able to go to a store while he was there and buy a new head. A few years earlier, Aunt Kirsten and I rode a train together. I played with my doll and innocently, but much to Kirsten's embarrassment, chattered away with a fellow passenger, "A German doctor gave me this doll, but it's all right because he's a nice German." The atmosphere in the compartment instantly turned chilly. Danes were not very friendly to a young woman who would let a 'nice' German give a fancy present to her daughter, as they naturally assumed I was. They probably also thought me of dubious parentage.

Far returned from Germany with a cage of infected mice. "Well, did you find a head for my doll?" I demanded.

Patiently he tried to explain the impossibility of granting my request and to describe some of the devastation in that industrial city; but that the invader could be suffering was beyond my ken. We might have a few shortages and be woken by air-raid sirens, but that was nothing compared to what Far had seen in Germany. What he had seen was nothing compared to the horrors to come to that enemy in defeat. One by one, his German colleagues in Frankfurt had pulled him off into a quiet corner to explain they were not responsible for all this insanity. Mostly they needed someone to talk to, someone they could trust. They didn't dare talk to each other. "When I asked them about the hole in the lab roof, they explained that every time they fixed it, another bomb fell and ripped a hole again." Far told us. "They finally gave up and left it."

The broken doll and the roof in Frankfurt would both have to wait for the end of the war before they could be fixed.

In October, Far caught typhus fever. Usually it is transmitted by lice, but when he was transferring the infection from one mouse to the nostrils of another, the animal sneezed and confirmed another mode of infection. Far and two other doctors became ill. They had all been inoculated with either the previous vaccine or their newer version; neither was very effective. This was not the way they had intended to test the vaccine.

Far developed the characteristically high fever and was rushed to the hospital. Mor wanted to spend all her time with him and explained, "He cries every time they send me away." There was no one to look after me, so it was arranged for me to stay with my grandparents who lived at the other end of Denmark, just north of the German border. To get to Sønderborg, we would first have to take a train to Korsør on the west coast of the island of Sjælland, then a ferry across the 'Big Belt,' another train west, then change to the southbound train. I was obviously too young to go alone. In the summer when we went to the train station to go up to the cabin at Esrum, I looked with wonder at the bedraggled city children being sent to farms for vacations in the fresh air. Tags with their destination written on them hung down from a button at the front of their coats as if these children were packages to be sent by train. I was thankful that we had an alternative in Far's eldest sister, Aunt Christel, who would take me the long way to Grandfather's house.

Christel was the only one of Far's siblings whom I saw regularly, and I adored her. She has always been 'Christel' to me, never '*Faster*' (a contraction of *fars-søster*— 'father's-sister'), as I should have called her. Nor did I ever call her by the family nickname of 'Bussi.' Because I was an only child, I generally addressed relatives by the same names my parents used: my mother's aunt was *Moster*— 'mother's-sister;' my father's other sisters were: 'Søster,' 'Ma' and 'Kirsten;' and his brother 'Niels.' It amused me to call two of my aunts 'Sister' and 'Me,' but that's what Far did, so the names seemed right. Christel had trained as a nurse in Copenhagen and now lived in the ferry town of Korsør. The other three sisters and brother all lived on the large peninsula of Jylland, to the far west; they seldom came to Copenhagen during the war.

Mor therefore took me on the train to Korsør, a couple of hours from Copenhagen. I spent the night with Christel, and Mor went back to the hospital.

The next day Christel and I went on her rounds together. She was the public health pediatric nurse for the town, visiting the home of each infant soon after birth, and then on a regular basis. She explained, "I visit until they're too big for my scales." These were portable 'Bismarck' scales, traditionally used by farmers to weigh produce at the market. Christel folding a diaper in a triangle and tied the ends in a sturdy knot. She had been to weaving school before becoming a nurse, and showed me how to make a secure square or 'weavers' knot. She then laid a week-old baby inside the diaper and fit the knot over the hook on the scales, slid a weight out on the bar, and held the whole contraption triumphantly aloft.

"Perfect baby," she declared, and turning to the mother, added, "Get me a cup from the kitchen and I'll show you how to measure things. And take out your notebook from three years ago." Korsør was a small town and Christel was the only pediatric nurse-practitioner. She taught health and baby care classes to all the school girls, who then later became 'her' mothers. She seemed to know everyone in town; they all greeted us as we walked by.

At another house a new mother said, "I have much more milk than my baby needs. It seems a shame to waste it. Can't I do something?"

"Do you know Fru Hansen?" Christel said. "She lives a couple of blocks from here and her milk is slow to come in. If you can help her out once a day or so." Who needed baby formula or a lactation consultant?

On Sunday Christel brought me to Sønderborg. There I stayed for several long weeks until Far's fever broke and he came home from the hospital. The aftereffects of his long illness were severe and recovery slow. He could not work at the lab for months, even after he appeared physically fit. He could chop wood at the cabin or move rocks down by the lake; but when a friend came to visit and they played chess, Far could not concentrate and, after a few minutes, the sweat poured down his face.

Far frequently spent evenings and Sundays playing the piano. Most evenings, I fell asleep to the faint sounds of a Mozart, Beethoven, or Schubert sonata drifting through the closed doors from the other end of the apartment. Far had taken lessons as a child, but his parents had stopped them when he wouldn't practice. As a result, Mor was determined that my talent would not be similarly wasted, and when I seemed reluctant to practice, she would cajole me by saying, "Please, play for me." This strategy worked very well, except that I never learned to separate 'practice' from 'playing for Mor.' Characteristically, she overestimated my talent and fully expected me to be a concert pianist or, even better, a violinist. One birthday they gave me a tiny violin and Far started to teach me the notes. I never liked the squeaky noises I made and quickly lost interest. I took it for granted that when I became an adult, I would be able to play the piano as well as Far, but knew early that I did not want to be a professional. After all, I was going to be a doctor, and who would want to practice for hours, every day?

During his convalescence, Far had more time to play. Although he couldn't work, his musical talent seemed to be located in an unaffected portion part of his brain. Mor urged him to ask Dr. Koppel if he could study with him. This was the concert pianist and composer with whose daughter I shared my wonderful teacher, Fru Holm-Johansen. With some trepidation, Far asked to be his student for a few months. Mr. Koppel must have been impressed with Far's circumstances, if not exactly his potential as a concert pianist, because he agreed to take him on. Far practiced with more diligence than as an adolescent, and reported weekly for critique and lessons. One time he came home with mixed emotions and told us, "I played the Beethoven Sonata all the way through without a single mistake, and then waited for Koppel tell me how good it was. He merely said a quiet 'yes,' nodded, and went on to something else."

During the last year or so of the war, Far went to work in the big infectious disease hospital, Blegdomshospitalet. I think he retained his laboratory job at the Institute, but during a war, there was little demand for standardizing sera for the League of Nations. There was also a problem because Dr. Thorvald Madsen had reached the age of mandatory retirement as director of the Institute. This vigorous man would have liked to continue working until Far, his protégé, was old enough to succeed him. However, Far was barely thirty when Madsen retired and was considered much too young. Far and the new director didn't always see eye to eye.

Denmark was just recovering from a terrible epidemic of diphtheria. It had been considered a children's disease and had been nearly eradicated by routine immunization of the young. Unfortunately when the disease became rare, those adults who had not been inoculated as children had no chance to develop natural immunity. Therefore this epidemic, with a case fatality rate of ten percent, was now spreading among unvaccinated adults. When Far was an intern, diphtheria was so rare that when a patient was hospitalized, the doctors were called to the ward just to observe a case. During the epidemic, there was no need for a special conference.

The large isolation wards at Blegdomshospitalet were normally used for children with scarlet fever. This disease was much feared because it seemed to spread so capriciously and was therefore thought to be highly infectious. In those dark days before the advent of penicillin, children with scarlet fever were sent to the hospital for six weeks of extended bed rest to ward off rheumatic fever and its aftereffects. Because of the supposed danger of contagion, they were under strict quarantine, even denied visits by parents. Visitors were allowed to stand outside the windows on wooden steps where they could see and wave to their children through the glass. Now these same wards were overflowing with diphtheria patients of all ages.

One day I was waiting outside for Far to finish afternoon rounds. In my boredom, I hopped up and down the steps under the windows, following his progress inside the building through the glass. I imagined being in one of those beds with scarlet fever, and Mor waving through the window for six weeks. Far, the doctor, would of course be allowed to come inside. Mor would probably talk her way in, too.

There was a big vaccination campaign to fight the diphtheria epidemic. My handsome father made a news film, shown in all the movie theaters, urging everyone to come to one of the public clinics. At supper, Far told gory tales of the long lines of people and his experiences of filling syringes and shooting rows of arms for hours on end.

A puzzled parent telephoned the Institute and asked, "It's been four days since my daughter was vaccinated. When can we take the needle out?"

Of course, I too had to have a booster shot. Far took me to his lab where I screamed hysterically while he prepared the syringe. In desperation he bribed me with a fur from one of the sacrificed experimental rabbits. Still sobbing, I perched on a laboratory stool clutching the soft skin and peering at the big world map on the wall. In the past, pins on this map marked all the places that sent sera and vaccines to the lab for standardization. Each pin had been connected with a thread, converging in a mass on Copenhagen. The different types of sera were coded with a different color pin. There had been everything from anti-venom against cobras in cigar-shaped metal tubes from India to diphtheria anti-toxin from Geneva, shipped right to where I was sitting. That was how I had collected all my exciting foreign stamps.

The news of the Allies as they advanced through southern Europe was very fragmented and had to be gleaned over the static of the radio broadcasts from England and Sweden. Since the map was no longer needed for its original purpose, Kai Jerne, who at the time was Far's secretary and later general factotum, used it to consolidate and decode the bits of information about battles. He moved the pins to show the position of the armies and the front. After the war, Taj, as he was nicknamed, received his medical degree, and continued the experiments on sera and vaccines that he and Far started in the lab. Eventually he received the Nobel Prize for his contributions to the development of modern immunology.

It was as if two girls were perched on that stool in Far's lab, a little kid protesting the shot and a preadolescent, puzzling over those abstract pin-soldiers on the map. This view was different from my experience of war.

When we prepared to go home, Taj took back the rabbit fur and I cried again. I thought it was mine. A bribe is not fair if you don't get to keep it.

One evening, I looked over Far's shoulder at the little marks he was making on a piece of paper. "What're you doing?" I asked.

He was studying the diphtheria epidemic among hospital nurses. Each case had been entered on an index card; they were stacked on the dining table. He was cross-tabulating the cases by date of onset and severity so he could look for patterns.

"You can help," he said, showing me how to read the notes from each case aloud so he could tally it in the proper cell of the table. "See, I make a little line in the table for each case. When I have four little lines, the next one goes across. At the end, the totals are easy to find, counting by five's."

"Neat," I exclaimed and grabbed the next card, enthusiastic about this new way of counting. "This one's a gra-a-a-vis." I enjoyed drawing out the Latin word, even though I understood that these patients had the severest form of the disease. There were a lot of *gravis* in the stack. The resulting publication was Far's first epidemiological study, to be followed by many more. It certainly was the first time I helped with Real Science.

EIGHT

Eosinophilic Granuloma

The spring of 1944 was marked by a dramatic personal event whose occurrence was independent of the war yet was colored by it, as was everything. It started just before the Pentecost holidays during what turned out to be the last year of the war. Denmark is not a particularly religious country, and the beautiful white churches sit in empty splendor on the hilltops; their lonely bells call to each other on Sunday mornings and say good night in the light summer evenings. Nevertheless, the traditional Christian holy days are faithfully observed as all work stops, stores close, and the people flock to the outdoors to worship the sacred sun, especially in the spring. Christmas is still called *Jul*, meaning 'wheel,' a symbol for the sun. In the middle of the dark-time, the still pagan Danes anticipate the soon-to-return sun-time. Even the streetcars celebrate the holidays, waving cheerful little Danish flags mounted on the front of their roofs.

The spring celebrations start with Easter and a week off from school. Ascension Day follows forty days later and then Pentecost vacation, soon after that. Flag Day commemorates the descent from heaven of the sacred flag with the white cross. It appeared in time to turn the tide of a battle on June 15, 1275 on a crusade to Estonia. Saint Hans Eve on June 23, the evening before the medieval feast day of John the Baptist, is the Danish excuse for celebrating midsummer's eve with bonfires on the hillsides and along the coast. The bacchanalian tradition of staying up all night and toasting the rising of the sun after the shortest night, started well before the Christian era, received its name during the Middle Ages when saints' days were celebrated, kept its spirit even through the somber Lutheran reformation, and is enthusiastically embraced by the secular society of the twentieth century. I never saw the bonfires, as they were not permitted during the war. Even though the sun barely sets and it is never really dark, the Germans feared the extra light along the beaches would mark the way for the Allied planes to lay mines in the Sound or bomb Berlin.

In 1944 Easter was late, three days after my ninth birthday on April 13. Pentecost was therefore not until June, and we headed as usual for Esrum. All spring I had been complaining of pains in my left leg. "It's just growing pains, you're getting so tall," Far, the doctor, reassured me.

Mor wasn't so sure. "I think I'll take her to see Ole Chievitz before we leave for the holidays. What else is a godfather for?"

Ole Chievitz, my grandfather's close childhood friend, was Far's godfather and Professor of Surgery at the Finsen Hospital. In the 1930's, Chievitz had volunteered with a surgical unit in Finland, fighting against Russia. He was a great man, but also a character about whom the family told many tales.

We knew him as a man of few words. In an oft told story, the surgeon's phone rang in the middle of the night. "Did you see a patient last night?" his wife asked the next morning.

"Yes."

"Anyone I know?"

"Your brother."

"My God! Was it serious?"

"No, just an appendectomy."

Another favorite story took place near the end of the war. Far must have known by then that Chievitz was in the Underground and important. The three of us were sitting at dinner and Far was as usual telling the happenings of the day: "And when I turned around, there was Chievitz standing next to me on the streetcar, looking right through me as if he had never seen me before. So I looked the other way and said nothing. I thought he'd escaped to Sweden, but I guess he's back in town and *incognito*! He was wearing different glasses and a strange cap. Does he think that's a disguise?" Far had quickly realized that acknowledging that he knew Chievitz might be dangerous for both of them.

I thought of the Chievitz I had met, a stern, impressive man wearing round metal-framed glasses—what I have always thought of as 'Lenin glasses.' Would horn-rims make him look different? Boy, was I impressed when I found out after the war that he was a member of the important Freedom Council.

Throughout the war Chievitz had been a persistent voice for resistance. The day of the occupation, April 9, 1940, he was again in Finland, leading a Red Cross medical team. He immediately came home to help the fight for Danish freedom. In May he captivated a large audience at the Student Union with a passionate and eloquent speech, an ironic example of a time when a public protest meeting could be held inside a university building while German soldiers patrolled the streets outside. In December 1942, Chievitz was arrested because of his connection with the Underground newspaper *Frit Danmark* and suspected communist sympathies. He allowed himself to be arrested, judging that the German authorities had little evidence against him and that it would be too difficult for anyone as well known as he to go 'underground.' After his arrest, he was put in a solitary German prison cell and then spent four months in a Danish jail. He was finally sentenced by a cooperating Danish court to eight months in prison, but was paroled the next day in view of the months already served and his 'value to society' as a doctor. Most of the court and the prison guards were his friends in the Resistance.

"When I complained that I had nothing to read, they gave me *Mein Kampf*," Chievitz told us when he was released. The Germans called him a 'blue-eyed idealist,' and did not realize that they had had someone much more valuable in their hands.

In February 1944, only months before he was to be my doctor, Chievitz was asked to be on the Freedom Council. This was the council of Resistance leaders who coordinated underground activities and essentially ran the country after the resignation of the members of parliament. A few months later, in June, he was again arrested as part of an illegal organization of surgeons, and again released when the Germans were persuaded that the group was merely an emergency unit of the Red Cross. He finally went 'underground' because his rising fame and another arrest might have had serious consequences for him and the Freedom Council. Soon after, was when Far met him on the streetcar, *incognito*.

This then was the doctor Mor took me to see during May, sandwiched between the time in February when he joined the Freedom Council and in late June when he went underground.

"Just growing pains," the busy surgeon said. "Let me see you walk."

I walked self-consciously down the long, gloomy hospital corridor, limping very slightly as the two grownups stared at me. "She's bowlegged," he explained.

"She's never been before," said Mor. "Her straight legs have always been a family joke. Like mine and Greta Garbo's." Mor stuck out one of her movie star legs to demonstrate.

"Let's see what an x-ray tells us," the doctor replied.

After seeing the picture, he changed his mind and said, "There is something here on her pelvic bone. We had better do a biopsy."

"He would never have listened to me if he weren't your godfather," Mor told Far that night. "But what I said about her straight legs, that's what made him take me seriously."

Mor had brought me to see Chievitz for the first visit, but refused to bring me for anything as traumatic as a biopsy. Poor Far was delegated; after all, he was the doctor and knew how to handle such things. The next morning, as we rode the streetcar to the hospital, he tried to explain what was going to happen. I didn't understand and didn't want to hear.

But when they put the ether mask over my face, I screamed, "Let's talk about it ..." as I went under. I had a nightmare that I was wrapped around the equator of the rapidly spinning earth.

"Well, did you have a nice dream?" asked the smiling nurse as I groggily threw up in the basin. Why did she think I would feel better if she denied the obvious and looked cheerful?

The next day, while we were at the dentist, Mor called Far to find out the diagnosis. She burst into tears of relief. When I asked her why she was crying, she explained that although I would have to go to the hospital for treatment, it was much better than they had feared. "We were worried that you might have to be in a cast for six months," she managed to explain. Cancer was probably on everyone's mind and 'cast' may have been a euphemism for amputation.

The diagnosis was *eosinophilic granuloma*. I like to think it was Far who figured it out by using his remarkable visual memory to recall a recent medical article from Boston, but perhaps it was Chievitz. A doctor had described the disease and reported success using radiation treatments.

The hospital of the Finsen Institute was an obvious choice for my radiation treatments, and not only because Chievitz was Chief of Surgery. Named after the Danish doctor who discovered the benefits of vitamin D and the role of the sun in its production by the skin, the Institute was a leader in all forms of radiation treatment. Those were the days when the sick were expected to stay in bed, preferably at a hospital. Of course, I couldn't easily be carted by streetcar to my treatments, so staying at the hospital made sense.

"Do you want to stay in the children's ward where you will have lots of company, or should Far arrange for a private room where we can visit you any time?" Mor asked me.

I chose the private room, not because of the visiting hours, but because I was afraid to have other children see that I sucked my fingers. I knew they would tease me; my schoolmates were bad enough, and they didn't know about my finger sucking. Only Ulla knew. She had enough quirks and fears of her own to accept my baby ways. Mor tried to comfort me by explaining that my adored grandfather still sucked his little finger, but I insisted that the ward was *out*. Hospital policy was reluctantly bent; but what else was a godfather for, even if he was Far's and not mine?

I was settled in a big, high hospital bed in a cavernous private room to be doted on by the nurses. Chievitz came on rounds. "I hear you won't let anyone take off the Band-Aid on your incision. Let me see—there, all gone. That didn't hurt, did it?" said the great man, grinning down at me like the idiotic nurse in the operating room.

"YES," I howled.

An orderly came to take me to radiation. "No, I can't get onto the stretcher by myself, I'm not allowed to walk." You would think he had instructions about how special I was.

The radiologist, guided by the surgeon, carefully painted lines in indelible iodine on the front and back of my left pelvic area. They studied me from every angle to get the lines just right. The radiation machines of that day could not be precisely focused and the doctors were afraid that the rays would damage not only the granuloma, but also my incipient left ovary.

Every few days I was carted off to Radiology, which smelled of ozone. I was carefully positioned, alternately on my front and my back, and the aperture of the machine lowered until it rested precisely between the iodine lines. Heavy lead pillows shielded the surrounding area. I had to lie there, very still, while the machine made a whirring sound.

The rest of the time I was in bed, trying to keep myself entertained. It is a mystery why I couldn't get out of bed, even if I wasn't allowed to walk. No one thought to bring me a wheelchair or take me to the children's ward to visit during the day. Far got up early every morning and rode his bike across town to visit with me before going back over the bridge to the Institute and his research. We played bridge; I struggled with one hand while Far played his hand as well as those of our imaginary opponents, Mr. and Mrs. Hansen. Far not only played the cards but invented long arguments between the imaginary couple. We giggled over those silly people as they bickered about who should have finessed when or trumped what.

"The nurses are going to ask you every day if you've moved your bowels," warned Far, the doctor. "Just say yes; they get excited about things like that." The nurses, of course, knew without asking because I had to use a bedpan.

Mor came every afternoon, showered me with books and toys, arranged to have my friends visit, and met my bored grumbles with her usual practical advice. Since I often slept during the day between visitors and had no exercise, I had trouble sleeping at night. Lights out was strictly enforced by the nurses, but they left a night light on in the ceiling, so they could check on me during the night. The light was too dim for me to read, but shone in my eyes and kept me awake. I gave up arguing the nonsense of all this, but found that if I held a little hand mirror so that the light reflected onto my book, I could double the amount of light, sufficiently to read by.

"Why didn't you tell me?" Mor asked when she found out. "I would have brought you a flashlight. I always read under the covers when I was a child."

After what seemed like months, I went home. Even then, I was not allowed to walk. I read and re-read every book I could lay my hands on, including those Mor took out of the library for me. She told me that we had to pay ten øre for my library card, a trivial sum even then. The prevalent social philosophy claimed that for self-respect everyone should pay something, so books were readily available but not quite free.

One day I was engrossed in *Alice in Wonderland* when Far came home. "That's a good story," he enthused, but then added in some misplaced fit of honesty, "It's all a dream, you know."

I was completely deflated and didn't even want to finish the book. I knew, of course, that Alice's strange world was not real, but I wanted to pretend it was more than a dream.

On good days, I was carried down to the yard to sit in my wooden wagon so I could play with my friends. They were supposed to pull me around in the wagon, but soon got bored. There I sat on my throne, feeling abandoned and frustrated. It was hard to be a Clara when I wanted to run with Heidi under the pine trees. I have often wondered why I didn't have a wheelchair. Was it a prejudice of the time that wheelchairs were for invalids, and my condition was only temporary? Or was it simply that they were not available during the war?

I think of the months that followed as 'The Summer of our Royal Progress.' English historical novels tell that when the royal purse was low, the king or queen declared a progress. The whole court journeyed to the castles of the royal vassals, living off their bounty until the guests had depleted the purse of the host and the privies overflowed. We may not have been a large court, but I was definitely a princess to be entertained. Mor, with her usual inventiveness, dreamt up a series of adventures.

First, she found an estate just north of the city where we could board for several weeks. It was near enough so Far could commute to the Institute by bike. The newspaper ad promised wonderful accommodations, great views, and swimming in the Sound. At the last minute, the hosts wrote us that they had sold their house and were canceling all reservations. When Far accepted the deposit back with only a minimum of fuss, they were so relieved that they invited us to stay as their guests until they had to move. The rest of their prospective boarders had not been as gracious.

The host turned out to be an entrepreneur, probably immersed in black market trading, and a finagler of the first order; at least, if one could believe half his wondrous tall tales of great deals and marvelous inventions. He had fallen on hard times because the war constricted investment opportunities.

His wife was even stranger, a mysterious gypsy with bangles, who had an eclectic taste in decorating, and kept chickens and summer boarders to help with the budget. I thought our hosts peculiar but enjoyed the novelty of feeding the chickens. Mor had a way of meeting the most extraordinary people.

Nearby, also on the coast, lived an older couple who were Mor's friends. I don't remember their name, but 'Silver-something' comes to mind. They had a small bungalow on a hill overlooking the Sound, with a path leading down to the beach. He had been a sea captain, then retired to become an adjuster of ship's compasses, and was now jobless because of the war. How Mor had met them, I don't know, but they were part of her people-collection. We went to visit for the day. I anticipated looking through the Captain's wonderful telescope at the ships passing through the Sound to and from the Baltic Sea. A short eight miles across the Sound was Sweden, that reminder of freedom and haven of the Jews. I wondered if one could get arrested for just looking at it. The old sea captain had had trouble with the Germans because of the telescope, and it was no longer on the lawn. The Gestapo was convinced that he had been collecting information on the passage of ships for the Underground. They were probably right.

Since our suburban boarding plans had gone awry, we retreated to our cabin in Esrum. I was still not allowed to be on my feet, so I could not bicycle there. My wooden play wagon was tied to the back of Far's bike, and he pulled me the long nine miles from the train station in Humlebæk to the cabin. Mor rode behind us, checking that all was well. A horse drawn wagon full of waving and cheering people crossed our path. "Do we know those people?" I asked, puzzled by their friendliness.

"Never saw them before, but people do that in the country —say hello to everyone," Far said. We must have been a bizarre sight; no wonder they waved and cheered.

As I sat there, bumping in the wagon and yelling a warning if it veered too far one side or the other, I figured something out. I had never been able to remember which was 'left' and which 'right.' Since my left leg was sick and I knew well which side that was, it was really very simple. Now I could call to my chauffeur, "Too far to the right."

On the southwestern side of Esrum Lake is the little town of Fredensborg and royal summer palace, famous for its beautiful gardens and spectacular view over the lake. If we rowed south from our house, we could look across from our side of the lake and see the palace, almost hidden at the head of an *allée* of stately trees. Fredensborg has a train station and is only about seven kilometers from the house by land, but we didn't usually come that way when we came up from Copenhagen. The bicycle trip from the station at Humlebœk was fifteen kilometers away, but easier because the hills were not as steep. Also, we had to change trains to get to Fredensborg, which was easy enough for people, but not very reliable when we had to send the bikes too. However, Far's vacation wasn't until July, so in June he commuted every day, biking to Fredensborg where he left his bike, took two trains and the streetcar to get to the Institute, and then returned in the evening. "I was in wonderful shape from all those hills," he liked to reminisce.

One weekend we borrowed a sailboat and sailed across Esrum Lake to Fredensborg. My wagon was brought along, and I was pulled along the path in the gardens of the summer palace. We had a beautiful picnic and a lovely afternoon. On the way back, we were becalmed in the middle of the lake. Far paddled us home, singing beautiful songs as the sun set across the bow, and the moon and stars rose behind us.

On the last day of June, was the general strike to protest the early curfew imposed by the Germans. Far was at work. Mor and I knew there was trouble when he didn't return at the usual time, and we began to hear strange reports on the radio news. Usually this was heavily censored, but I believe the Underground temporarily captured the station. Hours later, Far came home and told dramatic tales of catching the last train out of the city, jammed with people trying to leave.

Later we pieced together one of the great dramas of the war. The Allied occupation of Rome, invasion of Normandy, and renewed offensive of the Russian army earlier in the month raised expectations that the war would soon be over. The Underground escalated their sabotage activities, and after every explosion, the Germans retaliated by shooting hostages or destroying Danish landmarks, usually by the infamous Schalburg Corps. During the last week of June they bombed the Student Union building at the university, as well as large parts of the beloved Tivoli, the historic park of cultural buildings, restaurants, and amusement rides in the middle of the city. The loss of the famous 'Glass' concert hall in Tivoli utterly enraged the people, but the Monday morning declaration of martial law and imposition of a curfew from 8:00 in the evening until 5:00 in the morning, was the last straw.

The strike started as a 'go-home-early' movement among factory workers in the city. "If we can't work in our gardens in the evening, we'll make up the time by going home at noon," the argument went. By Friday, June 30, the strike had spread to the whole country; the streetcars, trains, and ferries stopped running. There was violence in the streets. Far was happy to escape; the engineer on his train was also glad to go home.

In the city, electricity and water were shut off to force people back to work. People filled their bathtubs with water and carried filled buckets from the city lakes. Bakeries and food markets sold food at their back doors. People cooked community meals on bonfires in the middle of the streets and built barricades to keep out the Germans. Soldiers cruised the streets, shooting and killing, hoping to force the Underground into the open. The Underground avoided a hopeless confrontation and persuaded people to stay inside where they would be safe.

On Monday, July 2, the Germans gave in and by Wednesday, the strike was over. The Freedom Council announced in flyers that the curfew was canceled, the Schalburg Corps was leaving the city, and random shootings would cease. I didn't understand how that happened. Why should the Germans care that the stores were closed, food and water scarce, work stopped, streetcars abandoned in the middle of the street, lights out. How did that affect anyone but the Danes? How could an unarmed, orderly, polite people win against an army by just saying no?

One week later, as suggested by the Freedom Council, the city commemorated the victory with a two-minute silence at noon. Bouquets of flowers appeared on the sidewalks as if by magic, to mark places where people had been killed.

When we came back in the fall, the barricade in the street in back of our apartment was still there. We heard the dramatic stories of food shortages, bathtubs filled with water, the power turned off, shootings in the streets. We were lucky to have been safe in Esrum, but as usual, I had missed the excitement.

During the rest of the summer we made several excursions. We took the train to visit Far's aunt, Faster Mussi, for a couple of days. She and her husband lived on a farm, not like the little subsistence farm by our cabin in Esrum, but a huge estate. The city girl was impressed and I told Mor, "An empty wagon came into the courtyard pulled by four horses, just like Cinderella's coach! And imagine, it was only an ordinary hay wagon."

At tea, Faster Mussi weighed her toast. She had diabetes and had to be very careful about what she ate. I admired her scientific manner. I played my 'piece' for her on her grand piano. She must have been pleased with my performance because the following Christmas she sent me a volume of Haydn sonatas inscribed: "To Anne from Faster Mussi, Christmas 1944." I had to wait four years before my teacher felt I was ready for even one movement of one of those sonatas.

Next we took the train to *Myretuen*, my godfather Nielsen's 'Ant-Hill' where I had waited so impatiently for my parents to return from their pre-war travels. The house was far out on a long narrow cape of land called *Odden*. Mor had reserved a private compartment on the crowded train for her ailing princess. A strange woman knocked on the compartment door and asked, "May we share with you? My daughter isn't feeling well and there aren't any seats in the main compartment." Mor recoiled in horror and rudely closed the door in the poor woman's face. She was convinced that my immune system was so debilitated that I would fall prey to infection at the slightest exposure to unfamiliar germs.

We went to Myretuen because Far was to be godfather to a new grandchild in the Nielsen clan. They rented a hay wagon from a local farmer to transport the guests to the baptism, and we all set off to the little church. It was a merry trip, like a country baptism of a past age. When the poor horse struggled to pull the full wagon to the top of a hill, the men got off and walked, quipping, "Hey, that baby is too heavy; let her *get* off!"

At the church, the baby and I were carried to the front pews, the Nielsen's sat on the right, Mor and I on the left of the aisle. Sensing that I would be self-conscious at not being able to stand during the service with the rest of the congregation, Mor held my hand and also sat.

My parents had been married in this little church about ten years earlier by a friend who had just started his ministry there. Far's parents had disapproved of their engagement because he was still in medical school and "shouldn't support your wife on your parents' money." The facts were that the money was a legacy from Far's mother, tuition at the university was free, and Mor had a job and could support herself. "Besides, one bedroom at our boardinghouse was cheaper than two," Mor said. When I was older, the twinkle in her eye told me that they had only been using one bedroom anyway.

Far had written a letter home. "If you won't let us get engaged, we'll get married instead. You are invited to the wedding at Odden's Church on April 1." That day has romantic connotations, although also called 'April Fools' Day in Denmark. By ancient custom, a young man sends an anonymous letter to his lady love, enclosing a 'winter-fool' flower (a snowdrop). The lady has to grant a boon if she cannot guess her secret lover's name by April Fool's Day.

The year of their wedding, April 1 was also Easter Sunday. Mor called Myretuen the night before the ceremony to wish the Nielsen family a Happy Easter, forgetting that the country operator would announce where she was calling from. "What on earth are you doing way out here?" Mrs. Nielsen asked.

"I'm getting married tomorrow," Mor confessed sheepishly.

The whole Nielsen family showed up at the church; the Ipsen clan was not represented. At the end of the Easter service, the congregation was invited to stay for the wedding. Mor carried an armful of long stemmed red roses. "My knees shook so hard I could hardly stand, but Far held my hand and steadied me," she whispered to me as she held my hand in the same pew, ten years later.

I loved the story and asked her to tell it over and over. No one had as wonderful and romantic parents! I dreamt of having red roses at my wedding.

My parents' rings were simple silver bands. "That's all we could afford," Mor said. "But no one was sure on which hand they were worn."

"If anyone asks, we'll just say that's how we do it here on Odden," declared the inexperienced minister.

In Denmark, the woman traditionally wears her ring on the left hand during the engagement; then it's switched to the right during the wedding ceremony.

"Ips lost his two weeks later; he kept fiddling with it," Mor would add when telling the story. "He's always fiddling and is so absent minded he looses everything."

Of course the wedding party went back to Myretuen for a celebration. A year and thirteen days later I was born. Ten years later, there we were for the baptism and there was the whole tale recorded in the Nielsen guest book. I otherwise hated that book because I was expected to write or paint something creative in it whenever I was a guest.

This visit to Myretuen was different from usual. Because of my illness, I couldn't roam the sandy heather-covered hills, look for deer skeletons in the plantation, nor hang from the rings on the swing set.

Going to the beach had always been a long trek for young legs, but having to be pulled over the rutted sandy path in a play wagon was fun for neither puller nor passenger. The best fun had always been to dive into the big waves during windy weather; just lying on the beach was too tame. However, the sun and air at the beach were just what I needed. A photo, taken before we left Copenhagen, shows me pale and wan from living indoors. Next to that in the album is a picture taken at Myreturen; I am by a sand castle, lying down to be sure, but the picture of health. Even the black-and-white print shows that my cheeks are full, my skin tanned, my short hair whipped by the wind.

I was teased about sucking my fingers. I had a slight lisp, caused by a wide gap between my buck front teeth. I had been blessedly unaware that I had a speech problem until one of the extended Nielsen family said how cute my sibilant 's' was and embarrassed me by wanting me to demonstrate. Fortunately, that same Nielsen uncle completely discredited himself when he went on to say how adorable my cheeks were, too. "And I don't mean the cheeks on your face," he leered.

We returned to Esrum for the rest of the summer. One memorable day, Mor found a horse and small open carriage for rent, and we rode in style to the beach at the northern tip of the island of Sjælland. I was even allowed to hold the reins on the way back.

Otherwise there were no further adventures. Far chopped down trees and read out loud to us, Mor baked bread, and I whined, "There's nothing to do." Far carried me whenever I needed a change of scenery, at great cost to his troublesome back.

Finally I was allowed to start walking again. This was a mixed blessing, since my muscles had weakened and I kept twisting my ankle. I would walk a little one day, twist my ankle, and then have to

A sick princess abandoned in the play yard, and the picture of health at Myreturen.

stay off it for several days until the swelling went down. Every night I wrapped my foot in one of Far's old ties in lieu of a bandage. The problem was aggravated by the growing scarcities during that final summer of the war. I had outgrown my leather shoes, and they were rationed and hard to get. Wooden clogs, still in use on farms, were adapted for street wear. One ingenious manufacturer used the scaly skin of the native flounder to cover the uppers of his clogs instead of leather. My feet, tender from lack of use, unfortunately rebelled against the inflexible footwear, and Mor had to use precious clothing ration cards for more conventional shoes. Eventually my muscles strengthened and I was as good as new again.

In August we returned to the city, and I went back to school after a long hiatus. That summer of the Great Progress had taught me many things. I became spoiled and self-centered because of all the fuss, but I also learned about love and how it can be shown in small gestures as well as great acts. My mother's understanding and inventiveness kept me entertained, yet made me conscious of her constant care for my welfare. Far's sense of humor and imagination never failed to delight; his vivid reading aloud of favorite books from his childhood enriched my mind and spirit. They both taught me to show respect and have good manners, but to use my judgment about silly regulations and other nonsense. Most important of all, I learned that even a defeated people can rebel against an army. I was probably at an ideal age to learn these lessons: old enough to be aware of what was happening, but not yet in the insecure and resentful years of adolescence. Of course, the closeness of our little family neither started nor ended that spring and summer, but it was intensified by a worrisome situation which had a happy ending after all.

NINE

Christmas in 1944

O ne day Mor announced, "We're all going to Farfar's house for Christmas! The whole family will be there."

Farfar, which is short for 'Father's-Father,' lived at the other end of Denmark. It was the winter after my illness and I was ready for more adventure. On the other hand, our usual way of celebrating Christmas was precious and familiar, and usually included just Mor, Far, and me, excluding the rest of the world. Whether I fully understood what it would be like to be in the middle of a large family and not the center of attention, my enthusiasm was dampened by the thought of a change in the established rituals.

Farfar lived in Sønderborg, in the western part of the country, very close to Germany. The distance from Copenhagen is not great, although about as far as one can go yet stay within the borders of Denmark. Today it is a matter of a few hours by train or car and ferry. As-the-plane-flies, the trip would be counted in minutes. But that Christmas (as it turned out) was during the last months of the war with reminders everywhere: German soldiers, identity cards, restricted travel, the possibility of danger, and endless hassle. Now it seems strange that my parents, Far's four sisters and one brother, not to mention assorted spouses and children, would choose to gather from all corners of the country that most difficult of the war winters. Everyone knew the war could not last much longer, so why then? I vaguely remember some mention that "this would be the last year we could;" Farfar would be sixty-five next fall, and he would retire and leave Sønderborg soon after. It certainly was not something we had ever done before.

It is not possible to travel very far from Copenhagen, located on the eastern side of the island of Sjælland without crossing water. Normally, a large fleet of efficient ferries transport people, bicycles, cars, buses, trucks, and trains in all possible directions between the hundreds of Danish islands, the mainland peninsula of Jylland, and the rest of the world. During the war, it was more difficult. We first took several streetcars, lugging our suitcases to the main railroad station downtown. The presents had been sent weeks before. The train crosses the island of Sjælland and normally goes right onto the ferry for passage to the island of Fyn, but during the war it stopped in the little town of Korsør on the west coast of Sjælland where Aunt Christel lived. This has been a ferry town since time immemorial in a country where saltwater is in the blood, and boats were, until recently, the quickest means of travel. We had to get off the train and were herded like cows along the tracks to the ferry by the despised German guards. Suitcases and papers were inspected.

I remember thinking with nine-year-old naiveté, "How dumb those Germans are—my heroes in the Underground aren't going to bomb a ferry with Danes on board!" It didn't occur to me that we were inspected to protect a shipment of farm produce from being blown up on the way to Germany. A bomb, timed to explode hours later, could be planted more easily on freight cars while they were on the ferry than along the way. The passenger trains were not allowed on the limited ferries in order to save space for these freight trains; the passengers served as hostages and bore the brunt of the inconvenience. The delay caused by having to walk onto the ferry and then onto the train at the other side was yet another reminder of war.

Was our ferry called *Broen*— 'the Bridge,' the traditionally tongue-in-cheek name of one ship in the fleet? Did we take a second ferry between Fyn and the island of Als where Sønderborg lies, or continue on the train across the long bridge and then down the east coast of Jylland? I only remember resenting being herded like a cow and the oppressive atmosphere of suspicion.

It was late at night when we finally got off the last train or ferry. Was that the trip where I got seasick on the 'Murmarkumark' ferry? The word (as I imagined it was spelled) is the name of the perfectly respectable ferry company. It still evokes a roller coaster, grumbly feeling in my stomach.

Far carried me off, half-asleep. "What do you mean we aren't there yet?" I complained, so tired, I cried like the spoiled brat I could be.

We got into a taxi for the last leg of the long trip. A taxi? Where did they get gas? Well, that's what I remember.

My grandfather's house was an official residence owned by the Sønderborg Hospital. He was a surgeon, and became chief of the hospital soon after the 1920 plebiscite that was supposed to resolve the Slesvig-Holstein problem after World War I. The Danish kings were hereditary dukes of both Slesvig and Holstein: districts of farm country with a mixture of Danish and German inhabitants, but historically considered part of Denmark. In 1864 Germany had marched across the southern border (then much further south). Chancellor Bismarck's goal was to take the land just to the north of the city of Kiel. The peninsula of Jylland is very narrow there, and he wanted to build a canal to give ships direct passage from the ports of eastern Germany to the North Sea. Later, in eighth-grade history I would learn about the battle fought at Dybbøl mill, close to Sønderborg. The unsuspecting, heroic Danish soldiers, equipped only with front-loading muskets, fought to the last man against Bismarck's modern army. The huge mill stands on a high hill. It is now a working museum; a war monument is in the memorial park next to it. Voices are muted, the awe and respect palpable as families come and remember their stories.

That long-ago invading German army was finally stopped further north, by the bridge to the island of Fyn. About forty percent of Denmark became part of German for fifty-six years. It was much more land than Bismarck had originally intended or needed for his project. Denmark was devastated, the defeat never forgiven and bitterly recalled with the occupation during World War II. Overwhelmed again.

In 1920 the League of Nations held a plebiscite, a direct election by the people living in Slesvig and Holstein to determine a new border and restore about half the lost to Denmark. The government, as a part of the repatriation plans, decided to build a modern hospital at Sønderborg, an old, historically important town just north of the new border. My grandfather moved there to help plan the new hospital, working very closely with the innovative architects. They saved enough in construction costs to add several modern features. The ceilings were kept low so that windows could be cleaned by stepping on an ordinary chair, baseboards were curved so that dust and bacteria would not collect in the cracks, operating rooms were built on the top floor and lit by large skylights. The top floor was a suite of surgical studios with Farfar's spacious and bright office-studio next door. Several generous residences with spacious gardens were built on the hospital grounds, including Farfar's house. The stories of Farfar's contributions to these design wonders of the hospital were always contrasted with his usual other-worldliness and legendary lack of grasp of ordinary money matters.

Here Far grew up and went to school amongst the local rustics. To my snobbish Copenhagen ear, they spoke a thick, incomprehensible country dialect.

Grandfather was a large, impressive man with a sharp nose, pointed chin, and small mouth. "All the Ipsens have small mouths," Mor would scorn, creating a bond between mother and daughter with our wide mouths and prominent chins.

Farfar was much loved by his children and grandchildren, as well as his many patients and the people of Sønderborg. His eyes smiled and twinkled. In profile, his body was shaped like a large S, with a huge stomach and bowed shoulders, his poor posture seemingly designed for hunching over his microscope. The microscope—the one Farfar carefully took out of its wooden case to show me—was used not just in the laboratory of his student days but also later for his amateur-naturalist studies. We looked together at the large notebooks with his precise drawings of flies, trapped millions of years before in amber and washed ashore on the beaches of the North Sea. He had a small lens attachment which allowed him simultaneously to see the flies under the microscope and the paper, enabling him to draw the minute details of eyes and feelers by tracing their outline.

Fafar, Dr. Johannes Ipsen, Sr.

I remembered Farfar's house well, although I had only been there twice before. One of my earliest memories is of my grandmother giving me a bath in a round washtub on a table in the bathroom. It was summer and I was only a little more than two years old. My parents were on their usual prewar summer trip to southern Europe to attend a scientific conference; the maid and I had been deposited at Sønderborg while they were gone. The big, dark, frightening, near-stranger Farmor seemed cross at having to bathe me. Did I think I was somehow at fault? The bath image sticks in my mind because it was an unusual occasion, but the explanation became a family story. It seems that an officious lady from the town had telephoned to inform the *Fru Overlæge* (the customary way to address the wife of the chief surgeon), that her granddaughter and maid had been observed in the company of a disreputable young man in a row boat in the middle of the harbor. Grandmother was not amused and sent the maid away. Hence Farmor had to give me my bath.

"Why couldn't she just have fired her, so I didn't have to deal with the ridiculous problem and pay two weeks' wages for no work?" Mor always complained when she retold the story.

The maid was the unfortunate creature who was scornfully remembered forever after as "Vera with the wet stomach" because she always managed to soak the front of her apron when doing the dishes.

The second time I went to Sønderborg was early in the war, when Far was so sick with typhoid fever and Aunt Christel brought me to stay with my grandparents. She and I entered the big house just outside the gate to the hospital grounds, but I couldn't remember it from my earlier visit. We climbed the stairs to a big hall with a tall grandfather clock and doors to all the bedrooms. Mine faced the front of the house and had a high old-fashioned bed. On the other side of my door in the silent hall the clock ticked loudly and chimed the hour.

The next night Christel gave me the bath, this time in the regular tub with hot water. Imagine, *hot water.* At home I had to take a cold water sponge bath and barely remembered luxuriating in a tub. Farfar's house was part of the hospital, and hospitals need hot water even during war time. The strange telephone-shaped hand-shower was at first a little frightening, but quickly turned out to be great fun for rinsing me and splashing everyone. After a brief stay, Christel had to go back home to her job and I stayed in the big house, feeling a bit like Heidi removed from her beloved Alps, but at least I had my grandfather.

"Anne, you must tell me if the change in food makes you constipated," Farmor said. This mother of six and nurse had a closet full of medicines; what would she do to me if I was constipated? I was used to cod liver oil from home (for vitamin D in sun-scarce Denmark), but didn't think much of her rose-hip juice (vitamin C) and was convinced she would have some other dreadful concoction for constipation. Fortunately that was never a problem. She hadn't said anything about diarrhea so I didn't have to tell her of the cramps I developed in a few days. I also managed to flush half of the huge bowl of breakfast cereal down the toilet every morning without anyone noticing. It might have been simpler to say that I couldn't possibly eat so much, but seven-year-olds have strange fears and I shied away from a possible scolding.

Life had not been easy for Farmor. Grandfather's adored first wife died in the influenza epidemic of 1918, leaving five children: twelve-year-old Christel down to baby Niels. Farfar's mother (Oldemor Christel) summoned her son to Copenhagen. "You have to find a housekeeper for all those children; ask that chief nurse of yours," she commanded.

Then shortly, another summons: "People are beginning to talk. Maybe you should marry Kikke." They dutifully married and spent many years together, apparently content, although Farmor always resented living in the shadow of Farfar's worshipped first love.

The intricacies of my large extended family were ever confusing but fascinating. Kirsten, my half-aunt, was born a few years after my grandparents married. At the time of my visit, I was seven and Kirsten only about twenty, but she seemed as grownup and distant in age as all my other relatives. She still lived at home and played the piano in the hall, the one Far had played as a youngster. Grandfather was reputed to be able to whistle any symphony, especially by Mozart, but he had never been allowed to learn any instrument. "He's too romantic", his stern father, the judge had said. Was that a nineteenth century reaction against *his* father, the organist? Farfar duly praised my efforts when I played my 'piece' for him.

Life was very dull for me in Sønderborg. The few children who lived on the hospital grounds were in school most of the day. Before supper I often went down the sidewalk towards the hospital, hoping Farfar would return early from afternoon rounds. There he was! I dashed headlong toward him and threw myself against his stomach, arms outstretched. Then I looked up. How embarrassing; it wasn't him at all, but some strange man, tolerantly amused.

After dinner we usually went upstairs where the three grownups smoked cigars, drank coffee, and played cards in the little sitting room. Even Farmor had a cigar. The dog had his own bowl of coffee and milk.

One evening there was a meeting in the formal drawing room on the main floor that was hardly ever used. The talk was very adult, something to do with someone, possibly one of the guests, who had escaped from concentration camp. It was very hush-hush and tense. I was expected to make the rounds and kiss all these strangers goodnight. What was concentration camp compared to that trauma!

Walks with Farfar in the blustery time between fall and winter were adventures, filled with nature lessons. "See that bird high in the sky? That's a lark. He'll be going away for the winter, but is one of the first birds to come back. He flies up in a spiral, singing the whole time, until we can hardly see him, then dives down to the ground-Let's turn over this rock and see what strange creatures we can find-

Do you know what this flower is? We'll bring it home and look it up in the book."

We carefully arranged the flower between blotting papers, and piled a huge stack of scientific reference books on top.

"Isn't it ready yet?" I asked every day.

"No, it will take several weeks before it's completely dry."

We made two little notebooks with cardboard covers that my mother saved for many years. One was for pressed leaves and flowers, the other for drawings of berries and things that couldn't be pressed or were out of season. A picture of mountain ash berries looked lovely in the big flower book. I tried to copy it into my notebook, but it was too hard for me to draw, so I traced it. "I wonder if he knows I cheated?" I worried, feeling dishonest; *real* scientists like Farfar or Far would never cheat.

I admired his tools arranged neatly on the wall, each hanging on its outline drawn to mark its place. "I have to be so organized, because I'm such a messy person," Farfar explained.

"You may borrow any of the tools you need from the wall or the desk, but *always* put everything back." Did I really dare use any of these treasures?

"Kiss Farfar good night. Now the other cheek, so Farfar's face won't be crooked. And the nose, just to make sure."

"Why do you always say 'Farfar' instead of 'me'? I asked. As an only child my speech was precocious and I didn't understand baby talk.

One morning I walked across the upstairs hall singing a hymn I had learned in school, at the top of my lungs. I pulled open the door open to the bathroom. There was Farfar sitting on the bowl, his pants down around his ankles. I stood there stunned as he grumbled at me to get out. I was troubled by the anger in his voice. He could have locked the door, I thought to myself.

"I heard you singing this morning; it sounded very nice," he said later, as if to apologize for his crossness.

It was getting dark. We were standing by the window of Farfar's upstairs study-bedroom, looking at the bridge to the mainland in the distance. "That's a pontoon bridge," he explained. "That means it floats on rafts." How strange, I thought.

He pointed across the garden to the army barracks: "The German soldiers live there now. Look at their flag, they don't even take it down at night, but fly it for the bats and the owls!" His voice dripped with contempt at the ugly red-and-black flag, the Germans, and their lack of manners.

Danes love to fly their bright red-and-white flag. It is cheerfully flown on Sundays, birthdays, when special company is expected, or when the mood strikes. There is even an everyday version, a long thin strip called a *vimpel*. It's convenient because not being a 'real' flag, it can be left on the mast, even at night. It's sometimes used at summer cabins to announce that the family is in 'residence.' The real flag is never flown at night "for the bats and the owls."

I certainly gained more from those five weeks than I would have learned in school back home.

Coming back two years later for our Christmas visit was very different. The house was filled with people and confusion. There was no big bedroom for me on the second floor, but a cot next to Mor's bed in the attic; Far had to stay down the street because there wasn't room for everyone in the house. I wasn't very happy with the arrangements. "Don't worry, I'll be back here first thing in the morning." Far assured me.

Cousins were everywhere, although some of the eventual fourteen of us had not yet been born. I was the eldest by several years. Søster was nursing her third, seven-month-old Jørgen. Ma's three were there: Marianne, Jens and thirteen-month-old Vibeke; two more were yet to be born. Niels left his pregnant wife, Marie, and four children at home, but came for a short visit. They would eventually have six girls. He was there just long enough to be included in a picture of the six siblings, taken by a photographer hired for the occasion. They look so young; the aunts all have their hair in fat sausages around their faces, just like movie stars from that period.

How could I have been so jealous of quiet four-year-old Marianne? Just because she was the next eldest and the only one old enough to be real competition for attention. Or was it because they lived closer by and Grandfather saw her more often than me? He kept calling himself 'Morfar' instead of the familiar 'Farfar.' A small but troubling sign that he was not just mine and had others to love.

The Christmas ritual was elaborate and well established. Grandmother and the two maids had been cooking and baking for weeks. I overheard a heated discussion between Mor and Grandmother about how many butter and sugar ration cards she needed for our share of the food. Mor retired with a headache; the two of them didn't get along well and Mor never felt accepted by her in-laws. She took a codeine pill and promptly threw up. At first she supposed that was a symptom associated with her headache, but soon realized that she was allergic to the codeine as well as her mother-in-law.

Liters of milk were bought from the milk man's cart that came by every day. We patted the patient horse while our pitcher was filled from big cans; no city bottles here. Was a horse-drawn milk cart still in regular use in the country or had the milkman taken it out of storage in response to the necessities of war? In Copenhagen, we often saw horses incongruously hitched to motorized delivery vans, otherwise useless because of the lack of gas. Here the regression to an earlier age was more complete.

The huge evergreen tree was brought to Farfar's library on the ground floor on the afternoon of 'Little Christmas Eve'—December 23. We were allowed to see it only while it still lay on the floor, horizontal and huge. Then the doors were closed, and we could hear sounds of sawing as some of the base was cut off.

The next morning there was a large poster at each door. "No admission, Nisser at work," said the caption under Farfar's drawing of little red-hatted gnomes. 'Nisser' are invisible folk from ancient times that live on Danish farms and in church towers. In a precarious covenant with their human families, they agree to bring good luck, do some chores, and suppress their mischief in exchange for occasional table scraps and porridge (especially on Christmas). In modern times they have become the Danish version of Santa Claus's elves.

Behind the doors there were sounds of soft squeaky voices, ringing bells, and occasional people-voices as Farfar and Far helped the Nisser decorate the tree. Our eyes and ears grew bigger as we listened at the doors and imagined the scene.

At home in Copenhagen, our little family usually ate dinner at six o'clock on Christmas eve, lit the Christmas tree, and then unwrapped our presents. I was expected to take a nap in the afternoon so I could stay up late. As if I could possibly sleep. Sometimes Far and I went to the afternoon service at the Church of Our Savior with the spiral tower, while Mor cooked dinner.

In Sønderborg, dinner was at noon because of the festivities at the hospital in the afternoon. The table was extended as far as it would go and overflowed with people and food. The traditional first course is porridge with a big lump of melting butter perching on top of the mound. Dark beer is poured over as a sauce. At farms another bowl is put in the barn for the Nisser. A single nut is hidden inside and a candy prize awarded to the person lucky enough to find it. During the luxury of the prewar years, the porridge was made with imported rice and the nut was an almond, but this year it was the more traditional oatmeal, the nut was a native hazelnut, and the butter was rationed. I never liked the dark beer and was happy to leave it for the grownups.

Farfar ran the show from the head of the table. "On the count of one, you may pick up your spoon, but don't eat until I count to three. One, two, three," he counted, slowly to tease. We all dug in, eating politely from the edge and not poking our spoon all through the porridge to find the nut.

"Who has the nut?" Farfar asked and then everyone echoed the question. No one seemed to have it.

"Chew carefully and don't swallow any lumps; somebody must have it."

Great merriment followed when the maids came in from the kitchen, one of them triumphantly holding the nut. Mor was relieved not to be the one to find it. She was often embarrassed by her perennial good fortune in winning the 'almond prize' whenever we had Christmas dinner with company.

After the compulsory nap, the whole family went to the hospital for afternoon rounds with Farfar. He led the procession like an emperor, his unbuttoned white lab coat flapping at his back like an ermine cape. The family court and a cadre of assistants and interns trailed behind. Each ward of the hospital had a decorated tree, cookies, carol singing, and hovering nurses making sure that the *Overlæge* and his family were pampered. At each station Farfar chatted with his patients while we admired the Christmas tree, sang carols, and stuffed ourselves. We certainly had no room for dinner.

After dark, we gathered in the drawing room back at the house for the traditional reading of a story—a classic about Christmas at a parsonage. I thought it very dull. We then waited in anticipation by the still-closed library doors. At home we always put the tree at one end of our combined dining-living room. Since it is traditional for children not to see the decorated tree until it is lit after dinner, I always tried very hard not even to peek while we ate. After the table was cleared, Mor and I would wait in the dark hall with the door closed until Far played the piano to signal that the candles on the tree were lit.

At Farfar's house, all of us clustered by the library and listened to more tiny Nisse-voices and bells behind the closed doors. I could see right through the wall that the room got brighter and brighter as each candle on the tree was lit. Then the double doors were thrown open to oohs and ahs as Far played the family Christmas carol. The music was composed a hundred years before by Great-great-grandfather the organist to words written by Great-great-grandmother Julie Ipsen. The decorated tree in the center of the room looked just like a famous illustration from my book of Hans Christian Andersen's fairy tales.

"First we show the tree; then we eat it," we sang in the words of a familiar carol as we joined hands and danced around the tree. It always amused me, the idea of eating a tree. But we almost did because the tree was covered with paper cones and heart-shaped baskets, filled with yet more candy and cookies. No wonder sugar and butter ration cards had to be saved for months in preparation for Christmas.

"It's nice to have enough people to be able to reach all the way around," I said to the amused aunt next to me. "At home there are just three of us, and we have to hold my dolls between us to reach around the tree."

There were so many presents they couldn't fit under the tree, but had to be stacked against the wall. The base of the tree was decorated with a snow village. Imagine having so many people that more than one present had to be opened at a time. That blue puppet theater with the winged horse is for me? Can we play with it now? When can we cut out the cardboard figures?

The confusion was overwhelming; I was used to a much quieter life. Too many presents, too many people, too much noise. But this was the best-remembered Christmas of my childhood and set the standard for all that were to follow.

TEN

L'Institute St. Joseph

Our Christmas reunion at my grandfather's house was a respite which helped us through the final stressful months of the war. The invasion of Normandy the previous June and the slow but steady progress of the Allies gave the Danes hope that the war was grinding down yet concern that we would be caught in the final battle. The inevitable finish also caused conflicting emotions among the Germans, and the tensions between town and uniform were palpable.

Although I had apparently recovered from my illness of the summer, there were several after-effects that profoundly effected on all our lives. Mor was exhausted from being social director and nursemaid to her ailing princess. Her emotional and physical health were poor. Partly because of the stress of the war, she had trouble sleeping and started taking sleeping pills regularly. Doctors didn't know much about addiction at that time, but the drug Far prescribed for her was thought to completely clear the body by morning and to have no residual effects. Eventually there were severe long-term consequences, which did not become apparent until many years later.

I don't remember exactly when, but it could have been during that fall that Mor was hospitalized for 'being run down,' or what we would now call 'anorexia.' She had been a fussy eater since childhood, when I suspect, she had gained her doting mother's attention by not eating.

She often told me, "My mor used to buy the very first tomatoes in the spring, when they were still very expensive, just to get me to eat." I thought of those wonderful, sweet, small, red, and juicy tomatoes nestled among the boring carrots and onions outside the little grocery store. Those first hot house tomatoes, not available during the long dark winter, were always eagerly awaited, followed by the tiny new potatoes and lush strawberries.

When Mor came home from the hospital, we plied her with rich desserts and custards to help her gain weight. Her doctor even gave her a prescription for extra ration coupons to enrich her diet. It is possible that she had given me some of her food rations, but I have no memory of food being truly scarce. However, Mor always made sure that I had my quart of milk every day, my afternoon snacks, and my evening apple. Small frequent meals were her weapon against my skinniness.

Since I was back in school after my illness and Mor badly needed to get out of the apartment, she became a Red Cross volunteer. The work was extremely important as she kept records of all the Danes in concentration camps. Mor set up a card cataloguing system, and helped ship packages of food and other essentials to the camps. These seemingly futile and minuscule gestures turned out to be crucial in the successful effort to keep many of our compatriots alive. Why that worked, I have never understood but suspect that Teutonic respect for order and the Germans' knowledge that they could be held accountable by meticulous record keeping, were part of the miracle.

We usually had some household help, or sometimes Mor's aunt, Moster Rigmor, came to clean and look after me. It became obvious that we needed someone on a more regular basis so that Mor could do her volunteer job. An advertisement in the paper brought some strange responses. One unprepossessing and surly girl was dragged to the interview by her mother. "She was only fifteen years old, totally unsuitable," Mor complained.

Finally, Frøken Lis Hoffman came to be interviewed. She was a tall, thin woman in her mid-forties, best described as 'a spinster lady in reduced circumstances.' During the war, her small independent income was inadequate and she had to find a job. Having her do light cleaning in our small apartment and keep me company after school was a perfect arrangement. She and I got along famously; she greeted me after school and we chatted while I had my second lunch or afternoon snack. Frøken Hoffman was much friendlier than the tight girdle which she wore because of her bad back. By coincidence, she had learned housekeeping as a young girl at Ulla's grandparents' farm, as was traditional in her youth. Later she had studied or worked in France. As I pored over her photo album from those days, I imagined a romantic tale of unrequited love with a dashing Frenchman.

"Frøken Hoffman, come and help me off with my snow pants," I demanded one winter day after school. She willingly came in from the kitchen and tugged at the heavy woolen pants as I sprawled comfortably on my bed.

"You know, 'Frøken Hoffman' is an awfully long name to have to call you all the time. Can't I call you something shorter?" I asked.

My request was rather brazen. In the Denmark of the time, even in my modern and liberal home, children were to be seen, not heard. When speaking to adults other than family members we always used last names and the formal pronoun *De*. Only children below confirmation age were automatically known by their first names and the informal *du*. Etiquette dictated that a change to a first-name basis was always initiated by the senior lady.

"Why don't you just call me Lis?" she answered kindly, without appearing offended.

From then on I knew her as 'Lis,' and Mor also changed to the informal address after a few weeks. Far, however, always called her 'Frøken Hoffman' since she never suggested otherwise; she addressed him as 'Doktor Ipsen.'

Just before Christmas, I started to complain about pains in my right arm. Another lesion was discovered on my shoulder blade, similar to the one on my pelvic bone the previous spring. I was treated with a few blasts of radiation. Since this part of my body was not as sensitive as the ovaries nestled close to my pelvis, the doctors could safely use a higher dose of radiation and fewer treatments. They feared that there might be more lesions, and I spent a day having x-rays taken of every bone in my body. My cranium was especially tricky. My head was strapped to a plate and I had to sit very still for the slow exposure of the insensitive film. Fortunately there was no sign the disease had spread to any other bones, and I never had another recurrence.

By the fall of 1944, I was in the middle of fourth grade at The Daughters' School. One of my class mates—let me call her Marianne, was the only child of the director of a prestigious museum. They lived in a large formal residence attached to the museum, and there were no neighborhood children with whom Marianne could play. Our mothers tried to arrange a friendship between us, and I was invited to her house several times. We ran freely through the large exhibit rooms, chatting with the guards who were more friendly than their solemn mien and forbidding posture suggested. In a huge workroom a damaged equestrian statue was being recast. We peeked in the door and tipped our heads way back, our mouths open in awe. The big horse was encased in wooden scaffolding, and I could barely see the plume on the king's helmet way up near the ceiling. It looked even larger and more impressive inside four walls than did the original in the square outside.

The family had a little private garden in back of the museum where we fed the pigeons which flew in from the square. Their formal living room was as palatial as the exhibit rooms and had the same glossy parquet floors.

"Lis says that in France, the maids wax and shine floors like these by tying thick cloths to their feet and skating across the wood," I told my friend under the disapproving eye of her stuffy mother. "Maybe we could try that." Although I was in awe of the famous place, I wanted to liven things up a little. Poor Marianne, what a way to live. No wonder she was a bully at school.

After tea we ran out of things to explore. Marianne had an argument with her mother and threw herself to the floor screaming. I stood there, embarrassed and not knowing what to do, hoping it would soon be time for me to leave. I understood about arguing with a mother, but felt we were a little too old for tantrums on the floor.

"I'm never going there again," I swore when I got home.

Unfortunately Marianne was one of the class leaders in my very small grade; she now became my enemy. I was easy to bully and became miserable at school. At first when I returned after my illness and was still not allowed to walk too far, Mor had pulled me to school in the wooden wagon. I finally refused to be a spectacle and walked by my self. Even then, I couldn't run around at recess or participate in gym class. Actually I was glad of the restriction on gym because then I didn't have to take a shower afterwards—a *cold* shower. My classmates resented these constant reminders that I was supposed to have special treatment and I felt apart from them.

We only had a short time for lunch and I was a slow eater. Marianne hid my sandwich so I couldn't finish in time. I complained bitterly at home. One day Mor waited around the corner from the school as we were dismissed at two o'clock. She watched as I came down the steps and several classmates ran by grabbing my hat.

"Naa na naa na naa na," they chanted in the international language of mean children and tossed my hat back and forth while I stood there helplessly.

"That's it, you are not going back there," said Mor, a furious lioness protecting her cub as she screamed at the nasty children, grabbed my arm, and pulled me home.

This was the last straw. I think Mor had been planning a change of school for some time because arrangements were made remarkably quickly, and after Christmas I was to start at the 'French School.' Mor had wanted me to go there when I first began school, but I had been too young to take the streetcar by myself to the other side of town. There were two large private girls' schools in town: Zahles and the French School. Zahles was the choice of the royal family. Mor was a snob, but a socialist, who didn't want me to have to compete with chauffeur-driven princesses.

"Besides, the nuns will be kind," Mor decided.

Denmark is overwhelmingly Lutheran although people are free to belong to other religions, including the Roman Catholic Church and Judaism. Under freedom of religion laws, each taxpayer designates which religion will receive proportional state support, including, I suppose, none at all. These arrangements have evolved over time and are taken for granted, although they seem very strange to the American trained to regard separation of Church and State as fundamental to a free society. There is also heavy state support of private schools. The intention is to allow parents freedom of choice and to stimulate diversity of educational philosophy. Quality of education is ensured by the Ministry of Education which standardizes and supervises the examinations which determine progression from elementary to middle school, to gymnasium, and finally to the university.

The French School was founded by the French order of St. Joseph to provide a haven of Roman Catholic education in heavily Lutheran Denmark. Because of the war, I suppose, they increasingly relied on government funds, and the school was required to accept Lutheran as well as Catholic girls. I was asked to bring in my baptismal certificate, to prove that I was at least a Christian. I wondered what would have happened if I had not been baptized. Or what if I had been Jewish?

The school's real name was *L'Institute St. Joseph*, as I soon learned to say with flourish. It was known as 'French' not only because of the order of nuns, but because originally most classes were taught in French from first grade on. When I went there, French was merely one of the many foreign languages we studied, and it was not introduced until the sixth grade. I always thought it ironic that English as well as Danish was taught before French in a French school. In other Danish elementary and middle-schools several foreign languages, especially English and German, were also part of the curriculum; however it was unusual for French to be taught before *gymnasium*—high school.

The German occupation government was disturbed that English was taught in all Danish schools and ordered the Ministry of Education to abolish it.

"Then I guess we will have to stop teaching German, too," the Minister said quietly.

"Well, English might be useful when Hitler conquers England," was the face-saving back- peddling.

Late one afternoon, Mor and I went to interview at the new school. We got off the streetcar and walked hand in hand down the broad avenue lined with magnificent chestnut trees. The massive brick building looked forbidding behind the tall wall. The iron gate was open but the huge building doors locked. Above the doors, "L'Institute St. Joseph" was carved in granite. Mor rang the bell, and a silent, black-shrouded figure opened the door and led us down a long, gloomy corridor into the Mother Superior's office, who was tall and imposing but indeed kind.

The biggest problem was deciding which grade I should be in. Because of the peculiar school year of The Daughters' School, I was only three months away from finishing fourth grade; on the other hand, the French School's year started in August, like other schools. The choice was thus between my dropping back several months in fourth grade or skipping ahead to the middle of fifth grade. Yet I was supposedly too young even for fourth grade.

"You may go with Sister Clara while your mother and I have a little talk," said the Mother Superior.

"You should call the Mother Superior *Ma Mère*, that's French for 'My Mother,'" Sister Clara explained as we walked back to her classroom. "Other nuns you call either 'Sister' followed by her name or *Ma Soeur*. That means 'My Sister.'"

We chatted about what I had learned in school and quickly established that fifth grade Danish was not a problem since I was an avid reader. Far's reading aloud had introduced me to most of the usual classics beyond my grade. Going through a story the second time by myself was much easier when I could hear his voice pronouncing the difficult words and getting me through the long boring parts with his humorous asides and explanations. During my illness I had swallowed every book that Mor or my friends could dig up. For Christmas I had received a three-foot high stack of assorted treasures from the used book store.

English was no problem either since The Daughters' School started this subject in fourth grade, while the French School started in the fifth grade and used the same textbook, so I was even ahead of my new classmates. History was new to me, but I could read the book and thus catch up. Arithmetic might be difficult; I didn't know what long division was.

"Let me show you how it works," said my new sister. In a few minutes she had shown me the tricks of separating the digits of the dividend into pairs, guessing the proper multiple of the divisor, and finding the remainder. This was a magic world.

"Do I have to go already? We're having so much fun," I complained when Mor told me it was time to go home.

"You've been talking for over an hour," Mor protested.

"I think Anne should try the fifth grade after the Christmas holidays," said my new mother. "She is a little young, but I don't think she'll have any trouble."

"It doesn't matter," Mor explained. "Right after the war we're going to America, so she'll lose a year and have to go back a grade anyway when we return to Denmark."

It didn't quite turn out that way, but we couldn't have known that.

Our homeroom teacher was Sister Marie Agnes, who also taught English and was the assistant to the Mother Superior. I suppose she was in her fifties but her lined face seemed ancient, framed by the white linen wimple and black veil. The front of her chest was covered by the white semi-circle of her stiff collar. Her habit was of thin black wool with a pleated bodice; long, full sleeves over the knit jersey which covered her arms; and a long, full skirt with innumerable hidden pockets. At rest she clasped her arms together in front of her waist, hiding them in the full sleeves like a mandarin scholar in his black silk gown. She towered over us from the lectern on her desk, which was placed squarely on the podium in front of the blackboard.

As she took attendance or made notations in the large register grading each student's recitation, she smiled at us benignly, peering through her glasses with lenses as thick as the bottoms of soda bottles. She was so near-sighted that she had to bend within inches of the page to see our names. I was long-since an adult before I realized that she probably couldn't see anyone's face beyond the first row. Her students never thought to misbehave, except the girl who sat in the first row right below Ma Soeur's desk. She giggled quietly as she propped the open English text against the lectern where it was hidden from view, and flawlessly recited the vocabulary words for the day.

Ma Soeur called me to the front of the class, "Tell us about this song in the book." To the rest of the class she explained, "Anne is several chapters ahead of us and can translate."

I should have been terrified, but instead I confidently sang about old King Cole and his merry old soul to the room full of strange faces. They seemed impressed. "And they told me I couldn't sing," I thought to myself as I sat down, satisfied with my performance.

Sister Marie Agnes was aware of the awe she inspired, but used her power with humor. A girl had the hiccups. "Come up here," she said sternly. "Give me your right thumb," she added severely. Her eyes were huge behind the distorting lenses as she fixed them on the shaking girl.

Then, breaking into a triumphant smile, she said, "Look, your hiccups are all gone. You may sit down."

Formidable as she was, she was always kind to me, and I developed a great affection for her as well as respect. Knowing of my troubles at my last school, she was very concerned that I should settle in. "Let me know if you don't have enough time to eat your lunch," she said to me privately. I heard a message of care and felt at home.

I learned her secret for creating acceptance in her classroom when she announced that another new girl was expected. "Next week, Susanne will be joining us," Ma Soeur said. "She has a condition that makes her shake her head slightly from side to side. She's very self-conscious about it, so don't make her feel worse by paying any attention. As soon as you get to know her, you'll forget that she's a little different."

Susanne was quickly accepted without teasing. Frankness and preparation can forestall much trouble.

My day began with several streetcar rides. I had a monthly fare card, like a grown-up. Mor and I went to a booth by one of the canals to pay for the first month. A surly man in a conductor's uniform glared at us through a window in his tiny kiosk. He showed us a map of the various routes as if he were doing us a favor, and we picked the one that included the French School. He then put together a little folder with the route highlighted on one side and my picture glued to the other. There was a little clear pocket where the receipt for the month was inserted. At the end of each month I had to report to this ogre in his cave and pay for the next month.

I caught the No. 9 streetcar on Market Street which took me over the drawbridge and then to the King's New Square. There I waited on the steps of the Royal Theater between the statues of Drachman and Øgenslager, nineteenth century poets and playwrights, for the No. 1 or 6 streetcar. I could also take the No. 9 all the way to the East

Railroad Station and change there, but it was more fun to wait by the Royal Theater. The streetcar stopped at the East Railroad Station, where we usually caught the train to go to the country, then it ambled down the broad avenue of East Bridge Street where the French School hid behind its wall. This part of the street was later renamed for the martyred head of the United Nations, Dag Hammarskjold. It is also known as Embassy Row for the stately buildings on either side of the school.

This ride across town was long for a little girl not yet ten and on her own. I had strict instructions to talk to no one and not to accept candy from strangers, especially men. "Some people are sick and it makes them do mean things to little girls," was the cryptic explanation.

One day, on the way home from school, I gave my seat on the streetcar to a little old lady. "How nice of you, little girl," said the woman, who was no taller than I. "Have a piece of candy," she added, holding the box out to me.

I didn't want to hurt her feelings, so I tucked a piece in my pocket, mumbling my awkward thanks but fearing to eat the forbidden fruit. The next stop was mine and I got off. After the streetcar went on its way, I furtively nibbled on the forbidden fruit, reasoning that the kind lady seemed harmless and that, short of her having poisoned the whole box with malicious intent, I didn't see how she could get me. She probably would have understood perfectly if I had said that I was not allowed to accept candy from strangers, but no one had prepared me for this contingency. Besides, candy was a rare treat because of the sugar rationing, and too tempting to refuse.

Once at school, I went through the big gates and to the playground by the side of the building. Students were not allowed to use the front door. The yard was divided into two areas, a little one for pupils in the lower grades where they wouldn't get trampled by the big girls, and the larger for the upper grades. Beyond it was a secluded garden where the nuns could walk and meditate. It was separated from us children by much more than a low fence; an invisible wall protected the private and religious lives of the nuns from the curious students. Those of us who were Protestant were even more puzzled by these mysterious women than our Catholic classmates.

Just before eight o'clock we lined up at the side entrance in rows by grades. The homeroom teachers led us to our classrooms in silence. I don't think this marching in lines was particularly French, but believe that most Danish schools of the time functioned similarly; possibly not as quietly. We met Sister Margrethe hurrying the other way. Each of us curtsied as we passed, a quick little bob that traveled down the line in a small wave. I soon mastered the technique of bobbing like this without missing a step.

In the hallway outside our classroom, we exchanged our coats for uniforms. These dark blue, belted smocks completely covered our dresses. They had little round, white, collars which were attached with snaps and brought home each Saturday for washing. Ma Soeur stood at the door greeting and shaking hands with each of us as we bobbed by her on the way to our seats.

We took out our little blue books. These small marvels of organization contained all communications between home and school. If I needed supplies from the school store, I made an entry in my book, which was collected by the class monitor in the morning and brought back at lunch time together with my order. At the end of the month, Far would look at the book, tally the charge, and send a check for the bill. Biweekly grade reports were also recorded here, to be signed by a parent. Yearly cumulative grades were sent separately. Notes from a teacher for home or vice versa were entered to be obediently handed over at the other end.

"Anne is late, with my knowledge," wrote Far one day when we had overslept and I panicked at the thought of the consequences.

"What a clever father I have," I thought. "He didn't even lie!"

A metal box was handed around in which to put our wallets, transit cards, and jewelry for safe keeping. Ma Soeur locked the box, and the class monitor brought it down to the office together with the blue books to be returned at the end of the day. We were allowed to keep watches and crosses, but money, for which we had no use at school, was an instrument of the devil, and jewelry was frivolous. The class monitor was Ma Mère's only concession to a new educational trend in student government.

The school was too big to assemble all of us for morning hymns, so we stayed in our classroom to say the first prayers of the day. Others were recited before and after lunch and at the end of the day. The routine was ordered and peaceful. Soon I was crossing myself four times a day as if I had always done so.

As at my previous school, we had a different teacher for each subject. Most of them were nuns and came to our room to teach. The exceptions were the Danish, history, music and gym teachers who were lay women of indeterminate age. Gym was taught in a large, airy gymnasium by a diminutive women who was also the director of a ballet school and drilled us in calisthenics. She always wore high heels so she wouldn't stretch her heel tendons. For music class we met in the big lunch room, sitting at the first few tables, near the piano. The teacher marched up and down between the rows, directing our singing by waving her pointed baton in front and her large derriere in back.

Between periods, we had to leave the classroom and go outside to play for ten minutes. By Ministry of Education rules, the windows were opened to let in fresh air and thus reduce the danger of tuberculosis. Since tuberculosis is spread by airborne droplets, this was sensible public health practice. We were allowed to go to the lunchroom for recess only in case of severe weather or a note from home, written in the blue book. If it was merely drizzling, we bunched together under the roof by the school yard door until it was time to go back to class. After the allotted time we were escorted back to our classroom by our teacher for the next period.

Lunch was brought from home. We lined up at the lunchroom door and handed in a little ticket in exchange for a small bottle of milk. A packet of tickets could be ordered in the morning with our other supplies. I suppose the milk, as well as our education, was government subsidized. Outdoors we played games, especially during the longer recess after lunch. We were supposed to keep the noise down and not run too fast. Our favorite game in winter was to make long slides of ice on the snow-packed cement, created by gliding back and forth on our leather-soled boots. Rubber boots didn't work, but rubber was an import so most of us didn't have them anyway. Ma Mère observed this hazardous game one day, and fearing that we would fall and injure our heads on the hard cement, ordered us to stop. She had the slides sanded, but after our loud protests, a compromise was reached. A student was placed at the head of the slide to allow only one girl to slide at a time, and one at the other end to catch her in case she lost her balance. Ma Mère even took a turn and saw that it was good.

I noticed little distinction between the approximately equal number of Catholic and Protestant girls except that we were separated for religious class. I don't know what our counterparts learned, but we were assigned stories from the Bible to memorize and recite; the instruction was very much as it had been at my old school, but without the evangelism. Ma Soeur who taught this class was a former

Lutheran. Since she had converted, she was judged able to deal with us Protestants without danger of polluting us or herself.

"I think you should all memorize the creed. It won't do you any harm," she decided.

She was careful to explain the difference in meaning between this use of 'catholic' and the name of her religion. Still, I wondered if the prayer was truly all right or whether the phrase "We believe in the holy catholic and apostolic Church" was some secret papist propaganda.

School normally started at eight in the morning and ended at two o'clock, except on Saturdays when we went home at one. Friday mornings, the Catholic students had chapel and the rest of us came at nine. Once our religion class went to see the chapel. It seemed like a small church, except that there were kneelers and lots of candles. Ma Soeur genuflected before slipping into a pew.

The only other obvious distinction between us and the Catholic students, was that sometimes a messenger would come into class, and the teacher would say to one of the girls "Father is free now, you can go to confession." Had the girl requested an appointment with a note in her little blue book?

This was indeed a new world; it was much bigger than my old school, but blissfully peaceful and wonderfully organized. How could anyone be a bully here? Nothing could go wrong under the watchful eyes of these dedicated women whose lives were devoted to this school and its children. The very bigness meant that I could sit quietly at my desk and hardly be noticed unless asked to recite in class. Although it was probably no more strict than other large schools of the time, I suppose some found the French School rigid, the nuns frightening in their strange medieval garb, and the many rules oppressive. Instead, I felt safe inside the cloistered walls, supported by the order, and free to dream my own dreams. There was much homework and we were called to the front of the room to recite our lessons. The emphasis was on memorizing: facts, the multiplication table, vocabulary lists, historical dates, and so on; but no one ever told me what to think. I was given tools, but interpretation of their meaning and motivation for their use was expected to come from me.

My feeling of security didn't last long. As the war front progressed through German towns and villages, many residents fled. These desperate refugees, especially relatives of important people, were sent to camps in Denmark, as far from the fighting as possible. Buildings were impounded to house them. Conditions in the camps were terrible and disease rampant. The few German army doctors had no medicines or equipment with which to help their people. Danish doctors were called to the camps, and the sickest patients swamped the hospitals.

I remember the discussions among Far's doctor friends of their ethical dilemma, "How can they expect us to help when they retaliate against Denmark by shooting doctors and nurses? We should go on strike!"

"We should not fail our Hippocratic oath. They're patients like anyone."

"What's a Hippocratic oath?" I asked.

The eventual solution was to assign the German doctors a section of the hospital where they could treat their patients.

The German occupation government realized that the French School, with its dormitory space, kitchens, and spacious classrooms, was ideal for a refugee camp. They simply ordered the nuns to leave. The St. Joseph's order had an additional residence on the northern edge of town, so this became their home and also our makeshift school. Because it was overcrowded we had to have lessons in two shifts: morning or afternoon.

My already long ride to school became even longer with an extra change of streetcars. The last leg was as long as my usual trip, so long that it went beyond the route marked on my monthly fare card. In fact the residence was just outside the city fare zone. I had a moral dilemma of my own, which was too trivial for the grownups to notice, but it bothered me. I could either get off at the zone border and walk several blocks, or stand at the back of the car and hope I could ride to the door of the school before the conductor came to collect the fare. I could usually see him coming and jump off the car as he approached. Getting off at the zone border and walking made the trip take even longer, and I was often late. However, it was by now an established principle that obedience to Danish law and order was a form of passive resistance against the German occupation. Personal morality was a rampart against the chaos of war: "We'll show them we're better than they." For some reason it never occurred to me to explain to Mor that I needed to pay the extra fare for the few extra blocks. A new fare card would have meant braving the ogre in his little booth.

My trip to school then changed from long to unreasonable, all because of a bridge. The channel of water between Christianshavn, where we lived, and the city proper was used by ships to pass from the inner harbor and the docks of the Burmeister & Wain factory to the outer harbor and on to the Baltic. Two drawbridges had to be raised to let them pass. Langebro—Long Bridge, had railroad tracks and Knippelsbro had tracks for the No. 2, 8, and 9 streetcars on which I rode to school. Both were main thoroughfares for pedestrians, carts, bicycles, wagons, and official cars and trucks. The older Langebro had a huge overhead counterweight to help raise the bridge; Knippelsbro was wider and had a more modern mechanism.

The Underground wanted to stop submarine-engines, manufactured at Burmeister & Wain, from being shipped to the German navy. This was a constant goal throughout the war. Following the earlier unsuccessful attempt by the English to bomb from the air, the Underground tried to smuggle explosives into the factory, but security was too tight. Since destruction of the factory was apparently impossible, they changed their strategy and tried by every means possible to hamper operations.

Langebro was the next target. They decided to disable the mechanism that raised the bridge because completely destroying it would only inconvenience Danish commuters without preventing passage of ships.

"They put a small amount of explosives in a railroad car, and carefully positioned it right under the counterweight." said Far, who, as usual, was telling us the latest Underground exploits at dinner. The lab was very close to Langebro; after he heard the explosion he went to see the sights and hear the stories.

"They had to do it very carefully in order to damage the mechanism and not the bridge," he continued. "German guards were standing right there but thought the railroad cars were merely being rearranged. After all, the railroad men were in uniform and looked official. The soldiers even helped direct traffic and watched as the engine was maneuvered back and forth. Then the Underground shot their guns into the air to warn people away. The Germans knew what to do and dove for the ground. The Danes, unused to the sounds of guns, had no idea what was happening and just stood there wondering what the noise was. Finally someone shouted, 'Get the hell off the bridge,' and everyone fled. The explosives worked precisely as they were supposed to; the bridge is still in one piece, it just won't go up!"

It took weeks before Langebro was repaired enough to be laboriously raised once a day. Both bridges were heavily guarded. Streetcars were no longer allowed to cross Knippelsbro; passengers had to get out on one side and walk across between the tracks, and then board cars waiting on the other side. Cyclists had to dismount and wheel their bicycles across. Larger wheeled conveyances were carefully inspected. The elderly and mothers with children were allowed to ride inside enclosed horse-drawn wagons that shuttled back and forth.

Mor and I crossed this way a few times. It was strange sitting inside the lumbering wagon, the canvas covering making it so dark I could barely see the huddled figures of the other women sitting on low benches on either side. There was some mystery involved. I thought, probably mistakenly, that the existence of this wagon and its cargo was a secret from the German soldiers. How could they not have known? I also thought that the canvas was supposed to keep them from seeing us. In reality, the covering was probably intended to prevent us from throwing bombs onto the bridge. Perhaps the authorities chose to ignore this minor, practical infringement of the new regulations to permit the transport of those who couldn't walk so far. Perhaps the hush-hush was merely because Mor and I were not infirm enough to qualify for this elder-wagon. True to form, Mor probably argued her way on because she and I were tired.

The next chapter in the adventures of the Underground involved neither well-guarded bridge. The ruin of a still-floating ship was docked next to Knippelsbro. Every time I crossed, I looked at the half-ship with wonder. It was literally the back half of what had probably been a good-size ferry or troop transport with many decks. A mine had destroyed the bow, and the stern had been towed to the dock. It was as if a giant saw had cut off the front, right through the middle of whatever cabins or corridors were in the way. How did it stay afloat? My imagination was kept busy.

One morning the ship was no longer at the dock, but had been sunk in the middle of the sailing channel. Now only the top deck showed above the water. Next to it, the masts of several smaller boats were barely visible.

Far filled us in with the news: "At dawn, the Underground showed up in several row boats, towed the half-ship into the middle of the channel, and drilled holes in the bottom. Then they towed some sailboats into the middle and sank them too, to fill in the gaps. The guards on the bridge just watched. Their orders were to guard the *bridge* not some useless *half-ship*. Initiative is not encouraged in the German army."

By this time, the trip to school took so long it was simply unrealistic. My formal education was once again interrupted and I stopped going to school for the rest of fifth grade. Between my father's illness with typhoid fever, my own granuloma, changing schools, and now the difficulties of getting there, I had not completed a single school year since second grade. It was one of the ironies of that time that despite the war, it was considered perfectly *safe* for a ten-year old to go across town to school every day by herself. The latest developments made it merely impractical. We were in the midst of a war and yet peculiarly protected from the worst of it.

ELEVEN

Far's Story: White People and Buses

When the war was drawing to its inevitable end, Heinrich Himmler, the chief of the Gestapo, secretly approached Count Bernadotte of the Swedish Red Cross to discuss the problem of the concentration camps, in an attempt to negotiate a settlement of the war. Bernadotte, working with the Norwegian and the Danish Red Cross, demanded release of all Scandinavian prisoners in the camps. Agreement was finally reached: they were to be transported through Denmark to Sweden and there interred for the remainder of the war.

The same spontaneous national and humanitarian spirit, which had helped the Jews escape a few years earlier, mushroomed: government officials, doctors, ambulance drivers, and volunteers joined forces to carry out the rescue operation. Because of the fragile health of the concentration camp survivors, medical personnel were needed to help with the transport, and doctors, experienced in cooperative team work and in dealing with emergencies, surfaced as the natural leaders of the convoys of buses that went down into Germany.

The official story of the 'White Buses' has been told many times in Scandinavia. What follows are Far's personal experiences, when he, as a doctor, became one of the 'people in white' riding these white buses on their rescue missions. He told the story many times to friends and family, and finally published it in 1990 in an anthology of essays by Danish writers. In 1992, Far and I translated his story into English so that our American family could read it. I include it here, in his own words, because hearing him tell it was an important part of my childhood.

Here then is Far's story—lest we forget.

These seven to fourteen days, which I will try to recall forty-four years later, were richer in experiences than most of the years of my life. The memories are like a videotape where faces, shapes, sounds, and landscapes change every second, sometimes unforgettably sharp, sometimes dim and distorted. The names of people and places are described as faithfully as I can recall, but times and dates are more blurred. Who, in April 1945 had time or peace to write a diary? But I remember it all started the twentieth of April because, ironically, that was Hitler's fifty-sixth—and last—birthday.

When I as a young medical student learned to write the section of a patient's chart called 'Obj.', we used objective, precise Latin and Greek terms to describe signs of illness in a human body and catalogue them in a diagnosis. When describing a sick society it is difficult to use objective language, but the diagnosis was a given: war.

My head was spinning when the buses drove across the border at Padborg that clear spring day.[1] Two days earlier I had phoned Juel-Henningsen at the Health Department to ask if it would be possible to collect blood samples from concentration camp survivors who had recovered from typhus fever, as they came across the border.[2]

"Collect them yourself," he said. "A bus is leaving Blegdams Hospital tomorrow morning at seven o'clock. Report to Niels Krarup when you get to the border."

Thus, rather un-heroically, I was shanghaied by the expedition. The next day we arrived, joining the dented buses with their wood-fired stoves in back.[3] They received a much-needed coat of paint, white with red crosses on the sides and roofs. Volunteers had come from all parts of Denmark, from Jylland and Fyn, as when the Viking chief called to arms, and their men gathered after the spring planting, manning the oars on the long-ships. They had to press on to make it home in time for the harvest.

Kjerulf, whom I knew from the time we were fellow interns at the communicable disease hospital, assigned me a bed in the barracks and added, a little absent-mindedly, but politely as always: "Excuse me, but I have to move a locomotive." The barracks were being heated by piping in the steam from a locomotive. He had become a heating engineer as well as a specialist in the circulatory system.

To 'arrange,' according to the unwritten dictionary of the day, had many meanings: to organize, buy, exchange, appropriate, steal, scrounge, etc. Mr. Jensen, manager at the Serum Institute where I worked, had arranged the supplies with the same precision with

---

[1] A small town in southern Denmark on the border with Germany.

[2] Far was still working to perfect his vaccine against typhus fever which had almost caused his death a few years earlier. Blood samples could provide important immunological information for the research.

[3] Due to the lack of gasoline, buses were ingeniously, but inefficiently, powered by large cylindrical wood-fired stoves, attached on the back bumper.

which he usually managed the chemicals, test tubes, microscopes, and rabbit cages. He was stacking some shirts on the shelves when he handed me a CB police uniform[4] with a Red Cross arm band. Later a colleague bawled me out, deservedly, since he had waited an hour outside the hospital that morning to give me a similar uniform.

Crossing the border, from Padborg to Flensborg, was familiar since I had lived for eight years in Sønderborg as a youth. During the twenties we often went to Flensborg for bargain shopping, but it was always strange to travel towards Dannevirke, brought up as we were with events of the war of 1864 and reminded daily by the sight of Dybbøl Mill.[5] Led by the snub nosed modern Swedish buses, which easily did eighty kilometers an hour, the Danish buses wheezed at thirty up the hills by Sankelmark, where the troops from Vendel and Copenhagen had formed the rear guard in 1864.

The convoy was organized. Himmler had assigned a member of the SS to each section. "*Ordnung muss sein*—we must have order," they were taught, but to them this was a liberty assignment.

"*Waren Sie am Ostfront*—were you at the eastern front?" I asked our SS officer, in German.

"*Ja, Panzer überall, vor allem Panzer*—yes, tanks everywhere, nothing but tanks!" and the booming music from Russian canons: "Stalin's organs."

Through Rendsborg we wheezed, past the royal-ducal hall,[6] across the repaired bridge over the canal at Kiel, which Bismarck had constructed to provide passage from the Baltic to the North Sea; the origi-

---

[4] The CB's—*Civil Beskyttelse*—were auxiliary police, the only police left in Denmark.

[5] Dannevirke is the ancient dirt mound, built in the ninth century across the peninsula, south of the present border, to protect Denmark against German invasion. In 1864 Bismarck's army marched northward and there was a decisive defeat and slaughter of the Danish defenders at Dybbøl, a large mill on a high hill near the town of Sønderborg.

[6] Before the events of 1864, the Danish king was the hereditary duke of this territory.

nal limited goal of his invasion. Up and over the peaceful wooded hills of Holstein.

Stop!

The smoke was pouring out of tanks and trucks on the crossroad down in the valley. Allied dive bombers had been there. A few final kicks to the kidneys of a fallen enemy.

We made a detour to a dense wood of beech and oak where we stopped for the night. Johannes Holm, Bernadotte's liaison and a specialist in tuberculosis, decided there were too many searchlights in the sky and too much gunfire for us to continue in the dark. A female colleague and I sat squeezed together in the back seat of a little passenger car; we could move neither arms nor legs. But having lived for several years next to the German barracks with the anti-aircraft banging away every time the air-raid siren went off, I was used to sleeping through noise. Our ten-year-old Anne always slept so soundly that it was a shame to drag her to the basement shelter.

We had a peaceful lunch at the edge of the park of a Holstein manor house. Miss Bro from the Aarhus School of Nursing supervised her lively students in making sandwiches. We had 'arranged' a can of real Brazilian coffee with the Swedes in return for a bottle of Aalborg schnapps.

In a chicken yard surrounded by a tall barbed-wire fence stood two bearded Russian prisoners of war. They were from a nearby prisoner-of-war camp and had been assigned to help the farmer with the work in the fields. They looked on with fatalistic acceptance. The wire was so dense that we could only slip a couple of cigarettes through the mesh. Their black eyes shone; they mumbled something Slavic.

Onward. Black and white road signs: Basedow 7 km, Wandsbeck 4 km, Hamburg in ruins. Detour. Around a walled-off part of the city where 40,000 dead bodies were fused in melted cement of the bomb shelters.

I was at the wheel of a modern passenger car, next to my companion of the night before; we were alone, bumping along a road paved with broken bits of brick. How had that happened? The rest of the convoy must have disappeared during the detours. Over the Elbe river. "Neuengamme straight ahead." What was happening at the other end of the Elbe? Does the German army still think that the Allies will hand them uniforms so the West can mount a crusade against the hordes of the East?[7]

The video tape flickers. An image of mounds of broken bricks. Probably Harburg. Then the landscape was spread out in the flat meadows north of the legendary Lünenburg Heath.

There it is! The white convoy bumped along bombed-out roads decorated with blooming spring flowers and dandelions, but no milk cans.[8] Little ramshackle sheds held women and children. Refugees in their own country.

Gray rows of barracks appeared, barbed-wire. The first concrete evidence confirming dim rumors of concentration camps. A Danish commission had visited our imprisoned police the previous fall. There had been a rumor of a scarlet fever epidemic; but the commission came home after having talked to a couple of chaps through the barbed wire. They reported that, on the whole, conditions probably weren't too bad. There were probably a few other camps around *das Reich* and in Poland. Our Jewish countrymen probably were not too badly off in Theresienstadt. A Red Cross delegation had been to Potemkinshow. They thought the eighty-one-year-old widow of

---

[7] In the subsequent partition of Germany into East and West , the iron curtain followed the southern part of the Elbe River. Only in the north, the Americans crossed the river by Hamburg, fought their way to the Baltic coast, and captured Lübeck during the last month of the war.

[8] A play on words: In Danish, dandelions are called 'the devil's milk can.'

Commander Schultz, my grandmother's sister-in-law, was pumping gas at a tank down there. Clara Schultz lived to be one hundred years old. We later found out that Dr. Holm rescued the prisoners of Theresienstadt just ahead of the advancing battles at 'two minutes to twelve,' against the advice of Count Bernadotte.

We stopped in front of the barbed wire. It was a little past noon. Talk and negotiations. Hundreds of gray men, Danes and Norwegians, stood at parade rest. They had stood there since six that morning. What is a well-trained *Obersturmführer* to do with men who have neither military uniforms nor a rifle to present? So he had exercised them with, "*Mutze auf! Mutze ab! Augen rechts!*—Hats off, hats on, eyes right."

Section after section shuffled into the buses. Dead silence. A command was called out, "*Funf und dreizig Stück per Wagen*—thirty-five items in each bus!"—Plus a doctor; how comforting.

Some of us knew how to do surgery and we had all *watched* operations. We could all write prescriptions: *Rx. In nomine Dei*—in God's name. Hippocrates said, "Sometimes cure, often relieve, always comfort." When had we been taught to comfort? I had served only two years at a hospital but eight among mice and guinea pigs in the laboratory; they were so easy to deal with. The nurses, at least, knew the contents of the first aid boxes.

The buses wheezed and coughed. We drove. A quiet murmur rose, louder and louder voices, laughter, cheers as realization set in. Northward! *Fryd og gammen*—joy. Farewell, Neuen-gamme.[9] The boxes from the Red Cross were opened: cigarettes, chocolate, crackers.

One clear image: the buses stopped on the meadows—for some reason convoys do that. Three little girls with white aprons and bows on their blond pigtails handed bouquets of field flowers up to the men

---

[9] A play on words, 'fryd og gammen' is a Danish expression of rejoicing; the concentration camp was by the town of Neuengamme.

in their prisoner's uniforms; daughters of the master race sent out to beg from their slaves. Generously, the men threw crackers and chocolate down into the aprons of the girls.

How we got back across the border to Padborg, I don't remember. It was dark. There was a meeting in the chief's little office. The air-aid siren went off. Dr. Krarup was speaking on the telephone to Copenhagen, "Please speak a little louder, *Hr. Departmentchef*—Mr. Department-chief. We are having an air raid and I am sitting under the table." He had a hard time fitting his long legs under the rickety little table.

We must have been sent to our quarters. There was a machine gun on the water tower. A fifteen-year-old German recruit shot at the Allied dive bombers, as he must have learned with his mother's milk. There was an answer from the air. "Ouch!" said a young CB policeman lying next to me on the floor. He had a superficial flesh wound in the thigh; a couple of inches from my head.

A temporary surgery was prepared. Thyssen, a young surgeon, rolled up the sleeves of his khaki shirt. A man had just crossed the border. After surviving several years of concentration camp, his right arm had now been crushed by salvos from the air. He cried. Thyssen amputated above the elbow. Outstanding job! A real doctor; a true field surgeon.

The next morning, the gray people massed by the waiting train. A voice over the loud speaker announced: "We regret the inconvenience, but last night the Danish Underground blew up the section of track between Aabenraa and Haderslev. Please wait for the buses."

Cheers! "The chaps are still at it."

After some time, the tired buses wheezed up and down the hills by Aabenraa. The streets of Haderslev were lined with flags and filled with welcoming people holding flags, flowers, cakes. The convoy stopped to accommodate the many diarrhea-plagued passengers.

A woman from the town stuck her head in through the open bus door: "Is Hans Peter Nielsen from Haderslev here?"

They shook their heads. She tried the next bus.

"Did she say 'Nielsen'?" said a voice in back of me. "He died a couple of months ago." What could one say?

It was dark in the big cold hall of the train station at Fredericia, ready for the bridge-crossing to the island of Fyn. The locomotive was hissing and billowing steam in front of the train; schedules were non-existent. There was a heated discussion with some German officers, something about two of the men having English uniforms. What the outcome was, I have no idea. Good English uniforms were valuable in the camps. An inner voice impelled me to find a telephone and call the hospital in Nyborg on Fyn. Surprisingly I was connected in less than ten minutes. It was nearly midnight. A student nurse answered.

"Can you 'arrange' breakfast for four to five hundred men from Neuengamme at the ferry harbor tomorrow morning?" I asked.

"I'll take care of it," she answered in a perky young voice with a sing-song Fyn accent.

The train started soon after. There were irregular stops on the way. Some men jumped off and ran home, others jumped on in order to escape to Sweden. No matter, as long as the final count was even so the man from the SS could deliver the correct number of *Stück* at the ferry to Sweden.

At the ferry landing stood the Nyborg Women's Club with steaming coffee pots and bread thick with butter. How had they 'arranged' break-fast rolls? My family was allotted only two rolls a month in exchange for two wheat ration coupons. Where did they find so much butter?

On the crossing from Fyn to the island of Sjælland, for the first, but not last time, I stood on the captain's bridge by the Island of Sprogø. The captain had called for The Doctor. He asked me whether we had any communicable diseases on board. I allowed that we probably had a half-dozen cases of typhoid and a collection of other salmonella infections.

"But that is against the State Railway regulations!" he exclaimed, horrified. I apologized and suggested that he have the toilets cleaned with Lysol and lime solution when we arrived in Korsør.

I sat with the man from the SS in the train compartment as we drove across Sjælland toward Copenhagen. I had asked my colleague Ernst Trier-Mørch what I was supposed to do with someone like that. "Fill the compartment with beer up to his knees," he had answered.

The man was reading the inventory list of the train load. He pointed to a name and said, in German, "*Dem mochte Ich sprechen*—I want to speak to this one."

I went along the corridor and found the one named. There was dead silence among the eight occupants as a pale fellow shakily stood up and asked, "What does he want now?"

The SS man, turned on a broad smile, put out his hand toward his former prisoner: "*Ja, jetzt sehen wir uns weider. Gute Reise!*—So, we meet once again. Have a good trip."

Oh yes, many would have liked to be going to Sweden.

A few images are missing, but by the next afternoon I was in Padborg, again. I must have repeated my request for blood samples, because Trier-Mørch arranged for a car, and we drove to the hospital at Aabenraa, where a man was recovering from typhus fever. I had had a laboratory infection myself and knew what it was like to have the fever drop to 98.6 degrees after a week at 104. I got the blood sample, but then couldn't remember why I wanted it.

We took the opportunity to make a short visit to my parents' house at the hospital in Sønderborg. Mother chaired the Women's Welfare Union there. A few days earlier she and her fellow members had prepared a hot meal for one of the returning bus convoys. Big pots of stew were ready in the morning and awaited reheating. The buses didn't arrive until late in the afternoon. She ordered four hundred and fifty pounds of precious lukewarm stew thrown into the garbage can. Sandwiches were served instead. As a trained chief nurse, she knew that staph, which we all carry on our hands, can change a wonderful meal to poison in a matter of hours, and delicate stomachs needed to be filled.

The results of a surgical intervention are easily seen, but it is strange that preventive measures never make much of an impression. Nothing happens—except for the expenditure of 'resources.'

A long train of cattle cars had arrived late that afternoon, carrying women from Ravensbrück, the witches' kettle for Europe's anonymous heroines. The intention had been that only Scandinavian women were to be sent to Sweden, but apparently someone decided to pour the whole garbage heap into the train. They had been transported for three days through northern Germany and Slesvig-Holstein without supplies. I didn't see them arrive, but was told that when the first doors were opened a gang of female hyenas threw themselves on a sack of rotting potatoes on the platform.

I saw them at the showers in the barracks.

Five hundred years ago Hieronymus Bosch described horror scenes of genderless human bodies on the way to hell. There in

Padborg stood such a line, as if on the way to purgatory; naked shapes, about to be deloused. Their dilapidated clothes had to be either washed and ironed, or burned. Lice have always been the worst enemies of armies.

"There is the daughter from Hvidsten Inn," someone said.[10] But all of invaded Europe was represented.

The masterpieces of Coventry, Dresden, the Vienna Opera House, and many other human works of art had been destroyed. Millions of men, women, and children lay in mass graves or under ruins. They were un-resurrectably dead. Why was the sight of these female figures, created by nature, sung about, worshiped and desired through the ages, so unforgettable with their half-dead, skeletal bodies? The sight of them erased the events of the next twelve hours.

Extra cargo cars were hooked onto the long train. Double-decker beds were arranged as in a twenty-bed ward with a central passage for nursing, feeding, and medical rounds. I can only remember that I stood beside a bed. She had black wisps of hair and was only half conscious; large eyes with black circles looked up at me from the white pillowcase.

"*Vous-etez francaise, Madame?*—Madame is French?" I asked.

"*Non, Monsieur, Lu-xem-bour-gi-en-ne*—No, Sir, from Luxembourg."

No alphabet nor musical notes can reproduce that soft, melodic, articulate assertion of a small, overrun, unconquerable nation in the heart of Europe.

The narrow passages in the railway cars where usually it is difficult to walk along with a suitcase, were empty, but in each compartment sat eight women, silent, tired. I should have worn a white coat

---

[10] Hvidsten Inn was the scene of an infamous betrayal and slaughter of an underground cell. The father and four brothers were shot by the Gestapo; the daughter was captured and sent to concentration camp.

because the dark blue uniform seemed to frighten them when I slid open the door. There were only short replies, or none at all. One woman sat breathing heavily, ankles swollen with edema. I suggested she lie down on one of the beds in back of the train, but seven pairs of angry eyes turned on me in protest. They were bonded in groups of eight. That was a condition for survival. The comb was the most important possession. Without a comb the last hope of feminine identity was lost. The woman stayed in her seat. Nine women died before we reached Copenhagen.

On the ferry, I walked up and down on the deck outside the restaurant where half the liberated prisoners were eating. Suddenly I felt an arm on mine. A little gray-haired lady smiled at me and said in clear Oxford English: "I have crossed the Atlantic, heaven knows how many times, but I have never enjoyed a sea voyage as much as this!"

We promenaded and conversed. I asked if she had had lunch, but no, not yet. We were by the Island of Sprogø again, which reminded me of last time I had been there, and I ran up the ladder to the Captain's bridge. Borrowing the microphone, I said in my best French, English, and German—in that order, "I would like to remind the ladies that they should, at their earliest convenience, relinquish their seats to their waiting friends."

Through a porthole I saw all the women all rise, one after the other in a matter of seconds, as if on military command; they shuffled out and the others shuffled in.

Just before we reached the ferry stop at Korsør, the head waiter came and handed me a bill for four hundred lunches. Eight hundred kroner! That was twice my monthly salary. I looked at him desperately.

"Just write, 'The Ministry of Social Affairs' and sign your name," he suggested helpfully. It was the biggest prescription I have ever written. *In Nomine Dei.*

How well the Civil Service managed without Parliament, ministers, and politicians.[11] I remember a department chief meeting us in Padborg who, single-handedly and at any time, could reschedule all the ferry crossings between the islands of Fyn and Sjælland.

On the train trip across Sjælland, I met a young, attractive girl with dark hair and red cheeks. She never answered my multi-lingual question about whether she wouldn't rather sit in one of the compartments.

She looked out the window, hopelessly and anxiously. Her kind were despised and rejected. Her beauty had been preserved with professional competence. Berthol Brecht said, "*Erst kommt das Essen, dann kommt die Moral*—first food, then morality."

The train stopped for a while at the edge of the city at Østerbro Station while the tracks to the harbor were cleared. To my surprise, my wife came into the train to meet me. I didn't think she ought to go into the cars with the bedridden, but she went through them anyway. She was wearing a new pleated, flowery summer dress, and her shoulder-length blonde hair was stylishly dressed. Looking pleased with herself, she strode between the beds. A collective sigh traveled along the car. Maybe I imagined it, but it was as if tired eyes lit up at the dream: flowered dresses and a coiffure still existed.

The train drove up to the waiting ferry for Sweden. It stopped on a side track, which meant that the exhausted women had to be helped down the big gap from the lowest step of the train, walk along the tracks, and try to climb up to the two-foot-high platform. The lines of women with emaciated or swollen legs and ankles, some with the paralysis that follows diphtheria after a few weeks, and all exhausted, were a heart rending sight.

---

[11] After Parliament had resigned in protest in August 1943, all matters of government, not controlled by the Germans, were left in the hands of the Civil Service.

A young CB policeman lifted a fourteen or fifteen-year-old girl up to the platform. A woman of uncertain age—between thirty-five and fifty-five—put her arm on mine, pointed to the young girl and said, her eyes shiny and tearful, "*Voila ma petite fille aidée par un soldat*—look at my little girl, helped by a *soldier!*" An impossible dream: a polite and helpful soldier!

I faintly remembered the fragile, pale girl from Padborg where I had listened to her pounding heart through my stethoscope. It was probably scarlet fever that had left bacteria eating away at her heart valves. They would only last about three more months.

However gladly I would have gone home to Christianshavn, I had to return to the border the same afternoon. A sick inmate from Vestre Prison had to be brought under guard to Frøslev, the clearing house for transfer to the concentration camps. Naturally, he had to be accompanied by a doctor. It would have been comical if it hadn't all been a dark, absurd confusion. I never saw the patient, but rode in a car following the ambulance, next to a German soldier in uniform. I must have slept most of the way and only dimly remember the armed guard who, according to regulations, had to accompany all cars and trains across the suspension bridge from Fyn to Fredericia.

When I was in the medical branch of the military service in 1936, we were told in our military courses that the enemy was expected to land at Vedbœk, just north of Copenhagen. (As it happened, they simply stepped off ships docked in the Copenhagen harbor, next to the statue of the Little Mermaid). The strategy was to hold the position at the next un-fordable millstream. Alternatively, the possibility that the enemy might attack across the border at Padborg and then march on to Copenhagen, was considered. The suspension bridge was prepared for explosives; however, the dynamite itself was stored twenty miles west of the bridge. "The station master has the key," our eager lieutenant of the reserves told us, thoughtlessly revealing this top military secret.

The camp at Padborg was in full swing. The assignments became more difficult since we were to pick up smaller groups here and there. Also, there was evidence that the Wehrmacht had started painting their ambulances and other trucks white. Single cars, not in convoys, were in danger of gunfire from Allied aircraft, especially at night. A lone Swedish ambulance had indeed been shot at, resulting in dead and wounded. Some Swedish cars arrived late at night; they had raced out of Rensborg.

"*Dom hängte up Julgranen*—they put up the Christmas trees," a driver complained to me in Swedish. The 'Christmas trees' were colored flares that were parachuted down from the fighter planes to mark a target, such as the town of Rensborg, for the slower bombers.

We drove in three or four cars through most of Slesvig-Holstein. A younger Danish officer had joined us; he was from the Underground and turned up in a Red Cross uniform. He was a nice chap. After a lunch break he confided in me, in a clipped private school accent, that he was frustrated at being unable to get the bus drivers going on command. "They are volunteers and do as they damn please," he said.

I lacked the proper military bearing. On a narrow road I had a discussion with an elderly German colonel, who must have served in World War I. The subject was the right of way: military column versus civilian buses. His gray, aristocratic Junker eyes looked at me,

"*Mein Herr mit dem roten Kreuze*—Sir, with the red cross," he said politely, unable to determine my rank by my peculiar uniform.

In some town or other, I quarreled with an elderly man who seemed to function as a traffic cop in the hopeless confusion. In his rage he grabbed the pipe from my mouth and threw it on the street. I picked it up and left. It's a bad habit, talking with my pipe in my mouth.

Rensborg was a smoking ruin where a couple of days before we had driven between neat rows of half-timbered houses. The prison was empty. I think our assignment was to pick up Danish citizens at civilian prisons, regardless of which laws they had broken. Not just Underground freedom fighters climbed into the buses.

Negotiations were simplified by a little good will in the form of cigarettes and other scarce commodities. I looked across the desk at a short, bald, persnickety prison inspector leafing through his papers. I placed a pound of Danish butter on the table.

He looked it over carefully. "*Ein Pfund Butter ist heute eine Mark, fünfundsechzig*—the price of a pound of butter is today one Mark and sixty-five," he said, obviously lying to prevent any accusation of bribery. He took out his purse and counted out one Mark and sixty-five Pfenning in coins. I put them in my pocket and he put the butter in his brief case. Only then did he remember that there was a Danish girl among the prisoners. She had had a job at the hotel in Hamburg, but had received a three-month prison term for stealing ten cigarettes from a German soldier, indubitably a major crime against the Reich. A girl of about twenty with wispy blond hair and a worn dirndl climbed into the bus. She didn't say much on the way home.

This description was supposed to be restricted to memories from those two or three chaotic weeks, albeit with some flash backs and associations. However, a memory from about a year later sneaks in. In March 1946, my wife, daughter, and I were on our way to the United States on the M.S. Falstria. In the salon sat a young woman, her fair, well-groomed head resting against her American husband's sergeant's uniform. Some young GIs were hanging on her every word as she told of her adventures in the Underground, ending with her imprisonment. She paused and lowered her blue eyes after she and I exchanged silent looks of recognition. One should not interfere with the happiness of newlyweds.

From the knee-high piles of bricks in Kiel there was a clear view of the half-sunk iron skeletons in the naval harbor. We had seen similar scenes in newsreels before the feature film. "News around the world: Pearl Harbor, December 7, 1941."

Lübeck was a depressing experience because I had fond memories from my school days when my father had taken two of my sisters and me on a trip through the 'Switzerland of Holstein.' I recalled the proud history of the area from when it was still Danish and back to the time of the powerful Hanseatic League. Now, the Church of Mary had been destroyed. Were they still there: the oldest Danish flag from the time of Eric of Pommern (King of Denmark, 1412-1434), the famous mural 'the Dance of Death from Lübeck,' the organ on which J. S. Bach played, having come on foot to study under Master Buxtehude?

A Swedish Red Cross station was run by a duchess: black slacks and black jacket under a braided crown of golden hair. Readers of Selma Lagerlöf's *Gösta Berling's Saga* would have recognized her as the perfect image of the chatelaine of Ekeby Manor.

In Lübeck I saw a strange science fiction-like scene. Two fighter planes followed by a white tail, streaked silently and with dizzying speed, northward across the blue spring sky. Only when they had almost disappeared over the horizon was there a loud boom—Wernherr von Braun's first successful jets. Too little and too late, although his unmanned 'doodle-bombs' had ravaged England until D-Day.

My last memory from that time is of a row of buses waiting in front of the Danish consulate in Flensborg. The passengers were a collection of women, children and old people from southern Slesvig; the interior of the stately old consulate building had been turned into a row of bureaucratic offices with stacks of official documents.

What a contrast from the twenties when the hospitable Consul General and his lively wife received me and their daughters' other school mates from Sønderborg in their tasteful home.

That day, near the end of the war, fleeing Germans presented old yellowed papers explaining that Grandfather or Great-grandfather had had an option of moving to Denmark from the conquered Slesvig after the war of 1864. Others sought to be reunited with purported Danish members of their family across the border. Lunch boxes were distributed in the buses. A twelve-year-old boy with water-combed blond hair approached me, bowed, and asked in high-German if he could have an extra box for later. I reassured him that he need not be concerned about his next meal. Denmark has always been hospitable to refugees, even when they are former enemies.

Two weeks after the chaotic pictures started, I was settled again at home on the fourth floor apartment in Christianshavn. Anne was drawing, and my wife and I played three-handed bridge with my colleague and friend, Niels 'Taj' Jerne. Absorbed in the game and Taj's amusing satirical remarks, we forgot to turn on the radio to hear the evening Danish-language news from BBC at 8:30. A few months earlier, the German jamming station had been blown up by the Underground; since then we had been able to receive the BBC newscast clearly. But we were not expecting any news from the western front.

How can one describe a noise that started with a murmur and rose to a crescendo to a thousand cheering voices? A jungle scream shook the air over Copenhagen. Standing at the window, we saw hordes of people, running, riding on bicycles, sitting on the roof of the No. 2 streetcar; a flood tide from Amagerbro Street, down Market Street, and across the bridge towards the city. It was the fourth of May and the surrender of Germany had been announced on the news.

TWELVE

May Flowers

The clouds of the final days of the occupation gathered in March and the rains poured in April. Peace bloomed in May.

The dark and dank winter months of 1945 were not helped by the increasing shortages and rationing. We hovered in front of the radio, trying to glean the latest news from Sweden and England over the noise of the Germans' loud static generators that jammed reception. I wondered why they bothered; we always found out the news anyway. At the end of the broadcasts from England there were mysterious messages, purporting to be family greetings to sailors at sea. As it turned out, these were coded messages for the Underground, with instructions on which railroads to sabotage or the location of the next supply drop. Fortunately we still had our radios, both in the city and in Esrum. In the early spring, the Underground blew up the jamming generators, so now the truth came in clearly from the free world outside.

The tensions and difficulties of the occupation increased. White bread was almost unknown; sugar and butter were heavily rationed. Mor had saved several pounds of butter in Far's freezers at the lab at the beginning of the war, and every Christmas she would take out some of her little hoard for making cookies. The rest of the year we had to make do with the ration. Mor decided that it was unfair that Far, who ate twice as many sandwiches as the two of us combined, should get more than his share of the butter, and she divided the ration into four little egg cups, saying, "One for each of us and one for cooking. Then we can each do what we want with our share, eat it at once or make it last till next time."

"It's full of vitamin A in the summer and good butter fat," Mor told me. She explained that 'winter-butter' is pale and low in vitamins because the cows are fed on hay instead of fresh green grass but in summer it becomes golden as the sun. She could not know then that all that 'good' butter fat causes heart disease.

But there wasn't very much. Mor learned how to stretch the butter by whipping it with eggs and other, mysterious ingredients. She became an alchemist in the kitchen, doubling our supply of gold; a household magician, using what she read in the newspapers and magazines, or figured out on her own. She made the stretching of what we had seem a game instead of a deprivation.

The thin wafers of almost used-up soap bars were broken into little pieces and soaked in water until they dissolved and formed a gel, which was used to wash clothes and dishes. I was fascinated by the thick gel which liquefied when I squeezed it in my hands, only to solidify again when left undisturbed.

Mor's experiments in preserving eggs in a chemical and salting away long rolls of home-made sausage were edible, but not very tasty. She got the pig intestine for the sausage skins from a relation-by-marriage of Grandmother's. He was usually our wine merchant and still occasionally found us a bottle of French wine, but this time, he had given us pig intestines.

Utilities too were limited. To save on electricity, we used only one lamp at a time. Before dinner we piled into the kitchen while Mor cooked. I warmed my hands at the radiator, tracing diagonal lines on the register grill set into the counter top, and Far recounted the happenings of his day.

There was not enough gas to cook dinner and also heat water for washing up afterwards. Earlier in the war, we had become very good at heating just a small saucepan of water in which to wash the dishes, and then rinsing them in cold tap water. Now gas for even a small saucepan was a problem; the resourceful manager of the apartment building allowed the residents to bring a pot down to the big furnace in the basement for a small allotment of hot water. For boiling the perennial potatoes for dinner, Mor found a little potbellied stove which we put on the back porch by the kitchen. She learned a tricky way to fold pages of newspaper into tight briquettes that burned slowly enough to last.

In the evenings, I did my homework at the dining room table while Mor and Far played honeymoon bridge. Mor used to send me to my room so the grownups could talk in peace; now we used less electricity by sharing the light. Far's hands methodically shuffled the cards and laid them out precisely, parallel to the corners of the table. Score was kept on the backs of envelopes in a shorthand notation of his own devising.

One night he told us, "Two Gestapo came to the lab today and demanded that I hand over my supply of experimental typhus vaccine. I told them I didn't have any left and that it didn't work anyway. We were standing right by the freezer filled with the stuff, but they took my word for it and left, frustrated."

"And they didn't get the butter that Mor keeps there for Christmas baking, either," I thought to myself, relieved that Far had not been caught lying to the Gestapo.

One of his doctor friends was shot and killed. He had been making an emergency house call after curfew on his motorbike. "He didn't hear the challenge over the noise of the motor and they just killed him," Far told us, white-faced.

An eight-year-old boy threw rocks at some soldiers and they shot him. "Be careful," Mor warned. She need not have said that; my friends and I stayed as far away from soldiers as we could.

At Christmas, Grandmother had told about visiting their summer house on the island of Fanø on the west coast. She had to get a special travel permit to go and check on it. The west coast of Denmark on the eastern-most edge of the North Sea was a possible, if unlikely, site for invasion by the Allies and was, therefore, heavily fortified. Most of the coastline is shallow with treacherous sand bars. The whole coast has only one harbor by the town of Esbjerg, which was built at the end of the nineteenth century for the thriving trade with England. The island of Fanø, formerly the center of clipper ships that sailed around the world, lies just outside this harbor, protecting it against the winter storms. The island, Grandmother told us, was filled with barbed wire and trenches. The Germans had paved the sandy road to the beach for their tanks and trucks. In front of the white dunes, where the family used to picnic and change into bathing suits, they had built ugly cement bunkers.

The Germans set up random checkpoints in the city. People had to show their identity papers and were sometimes searched for weapons. I don't remember ever being stopped, but heard the stories. A woman living on the ground floor in our entry of the apartment complex, was a midwife and a courier for the Underground. She was shunned by the neighbors because of her cover of being friendly with German soldiers. After the war, she shared her experiences with Mor who retold us her story:

"When the Underground called me with an assignment, the code was, 'Mrs. Hansen is having her baby; bring your medical bag.' One day, the black bag was full of guns; it was just the right size and camouflaged them well. I saw a check-point ahead and knew I could never pass inspection, so I flirted with an officer walking down the street. He gallantly carried my bag right by the line of people as we made a rendezvous for that evening. He must have wondered how a few obstetric instruments could be so heavy!"

Some time during the late winter or spring, before I stopped going to the French School altogether, I managed to take the examination which would allow me to graduate from primary school and go on to sixth grade in 'middle school' the following fall. At that time Danish education was separated into five primary grades, four middle grades, and three years of 'gymnasium.' Compulsory education ended at age fourteen, but most trades had apprenticeship programs which required specific courses in night school to reach journeyman and master status. Children normally started school at seven, spent up to twelve years in school and, if university-bound, graduated from gymnasium at nineteen after passing the 'student exam,' the only requirement for entrance to the university.

Since the assumption was that I would go on to the university, passing the exam for middle school was a necessary step. It couldn't have been too hard because I don't remember anything about it other than having to go to school to take it—and passing.

March 21, 1945, brought the greatest single tragedy of the war. Mor and I were at Blegdomshospitalet, the hospital where Far was then working part of the time. Possibly we were meeting him for lunch before I went to afternoon classes at the displaced French School, but subsequent events have completely erased why Mor and I were with Far.

It was noon and we were outside looking up at planes overhead. We seldom saw planes because the Allies mostly came at night, and the Germans had no planes to waste on Denmark. Then we heard anti-aircraft and saw clouds of black smoke over the city, followed by loud explosions, and finally the air raid sirens went off. We ran to the shelter for cover, but the raid appeared to be over except for the sirens, the fire engines, and the smoke. It was much worse than that other bombing from the air at the very start of the occupation, but at least this time we were together.

"The smoke is coming from the center of town," we heard, as the rumors flew.

"They've bombed the Shell House."

"The police barracks are burning."

"The French School has been hit—no, the one in Frederiksberg— the Jean d'Arc School."

"A plane is down in the park."

"God help us, what is going on?"

I must have had an exam because I still had to go to school. The three of us went together, uncertain of the exact situation. When we arrived, all was confusion and I was sent outside. I waited and waited, hopping up and down to keep warm in the growing dusk. Periodically, Mor came out and said, "We'll be a while longer." Finally we went home.

In the coming days, we put together approximately what had happened, but the final pieces of the puzzle were not known until after the war. The following fragments are from my memory of the time, but are nevertheless essentially correct.

The Shell House was Danish corporate headquarters of the Shell Oil Company. Because of its convenient location in the center of Copenhagen across from City Hall on a very large open square, it was requisitioned by the occupation government as German headquarters. On the top floor, important Danes were imprisoned as hostages to protect the building from attacks from the air.

With my limited, pre-war experience of gasoline, I had never heard of Shell Oil. I was always confused by the 'Shell House' and thought the very name had some sinister connection with war. At Christmas we had, as usual, gone to admire the traditional gigantic city tree. I averted my eyes from the other side of the square where the Shell House entrance was guarded by barbed wire and machine gun-toting soldiers. It was an ugly reminder of the occupation; not in the Christmas spirit.

Later we found out that a secret high-level meeting was to be held at the Shell House, and the Allies decided to attempt killing the attendees. Since the Underground could not get into the building, a carefully planned air attack was to be carried out. A full size model of the building was built in England and air crews practiced precision bombing, since conventional bombing from above would kill the Danish hostages. The planes were to fly very low over the square, bank steeply in front of the Shell House, and literally toss the bombs into the lower floors. If they could avoid a direct hit on the top floor, the hostages would have a slim chance of escape.

The main portion of the plan worked perfectly. The first squadron came in as planned and threw their bombs at the second floor level. The sirens didn't sound until after they had exploded. The planes were not expected and not noticed until too late; bombing of Denmark other than night-time mining of harbors was very rare, especially during the day.

I don't remember who gave us the following eyewitness account. It could have come from an Underground newspaper, the usual rumor mill, or one of Far's acquaintances. I like to think we heard it from Far's godfather and my doctor, Ole Chievitz. I don't think he was one of the hostages, but he certainly knew them.

"I was on the top floor in one of the cells. The blast threw me to the floor but also blew open the lock on my door. I picked myself up, walked up to the shaking German guard, and thundered, 'give me your keys and your gun!' He was used to obeying commands and so frightened that he instantly complied. I then unlocked the cells of the other hostages, and we made our way to the street. Fortunately the Underground seemed to be expecting us. They were shooting at the Germans, but had taxis waiting to whisk us away to safe houses."

Tragedy struck with the second squadron. It was not clear whether their target was the Shell House or the German army barracks at police headquarters outside the city. In making the low approach, the wing of the squadron leader's plane hit a radio tower. Apparently in a brave attempt to avoid hitting civilian houses or maybe in trying to save his own life, the pilot aimed for the nearest park and let go his bombs just before he crashed. The rest of the squadron, seeing a hit near an official-looking structure, thought this was their target and systematically bombed the four corners of the building. Tragically, this was the Jean d'Arc School. It was also a French school, run by the same order of nuns as my *L'Institute St. Joseph*, but located in one of the suburbs. Because the sirens sounded so late, the children were still in the corridors on their way to the basement shelters. Mother Superior was in the hall directing a class to "go down those stairs" in a corner of the building. Then the bombs fell; right on them. Ma Mère survived and later became my art teacher. I used to look at her calm face framed by her black veil and wonder how she could look so at peace. Mor told me she was overwhelmed by a feeling of guilt that her directions had sent her students to their death. How little one can tell from a face.

When we arrived at school, the Jean d'Arc nuns were being brought home to the residence. These were the badly shocked but 'walking wounded;' the more severe cases were brought to the overwhelmed Catholic hospital. Far immediately offered his help as a doctor. I was sent outdoors to wait where I would see none of the horror.

"Would you believe, they had to ask the priest permission for me to treat the nuns because I wasn't an approved Catholic doctor?" Far told us later, shaking his head. "Did they think I was going to molest them? Most of them were in shock and in very bad shape. One nun's legs were so swollen, I had to cut off her stockings to even see her wounds."

Mor also volunteered. For the next week we did not see her as she stayed near the bombed school to help organize the rescue work. The biggest problem was identifying the bodies of the children. The day's attendance books and even the enrollment records were destroyed with the school. Parents came flocking as soon as they heard the news. If their daughter was a fortunate survivor, they whisked her away to a safe place to recover from the horror; sometimes telling no one. There were appeals on the radio for parents to contact the school so lists of the safe and the missing could be compiled. Mor, drawing on her Red Cross experience of keeping track of Danes sent to concentration camp, set up a card index for each child and nun, color-coded according to the accumulating information. Finally there was only one unidentified body and one name on the list of missing girls, but the descriptions of their underclothing did not match. The colors were wrong.

"One of the doctors suggested that the color of the undershirt might have been changed by the heat of the fire," Mor told us when we came to pick her up at the end of the week. "We took a piece of a shirt from the missing girl's home, put it in a little metal container, and heated it in the oven. The colors matched perfectly. What a tragedy. The parents are devastated."

I tried to visualize the dead child and wondered why they couldn't tell who she was. I supposed she had worn a uniform smock similar to mine and therefore looked like all the other children. Or perhaps the body had no outer clothing and no face; only the puzzling undershirt was left. A child without a face was not in my experience; it was an image that I did not want to examine too closely.

On that March day we stood there, the three of us, looking up at the ruins of the many-storied building. Only parts of the outer walls were still standing; the rest was rubble. Incongruously, many of the radiators still clung to their pipes under glassless windows, the floors missing beneath them. The rubble was still smoking, the firemen still using their hoses.

"Look what I found on the ground," said the fire-chief and showed us a little glass bottle. "It's a bottle of mercury from the science room on the sixth floor. It fell all that way without breaking."

I don't want to remember the exact toll, but about a quarter of the more than three hundred children died, a third of the nuns. Two of the nuns were found with their bodies and voluminous skirts miraculously protecting their small kindergarten charges; like brood hens covering their chicks.

Mor and I attended the funeral service at the big Catholic church downtown. I could make no sense of all the chanting, incense, and Latin. I kept thinking how unfair the tragedy was. If one of the French schools had to be bombed, why not mine? We weren't using it. That the unfortunate refugees would have met an equally terrible fate did not concern me. After all, they were the enemy.

April 9, less than three weeks later, was Ulla's thirteenth birthday and marked the fifth anniversary of the German occupation of Denmark. The Underground organized a protest, a repeat of the memorial demonstration that had followed the violence of the General Strike the previous summer. I had missed that one because we were in the country and I anxiously awaited the repetition of an event about which I had heard so much. Mor made me stay home in case the Germans decided on reprisals, but I saw it all in my imagination. When the noon testing of the air aid sirens sounded, the whole city stopped in its tracks for two minute of silence. The streetcars, the horse drawn wagons, and the pedestrians just stopped where they were. People got off their bikes and bowed their heads. Two minutes is a long time. Even the German and their trucks couldn't move because of the stilled traffic, unwilling and frustrated participants in this passive resistance. Then the 'all clear' sounded, people picked up where they had left off and went on with their lives, pretending all was normal. Throughout the city, little bouquets of flowers materialized from unseen hands, placed to commemorate places where members of the Underground or other victims had been killed.

That same day, by coincidence, the first buses transporting the living skeletons from concentration camps came through Copenhagen on their way to internment camps in Sweden. The stories of the horror of the camps passed through the city, despite attempts to suppress the news. President Roosevelt's death three days later, however, was triumphantly uncensored. Mor and I were downtown shopping when we passed the huge black headlines at a newsstand. Mor stopped and exclaimed in horror.

"Who's Roosevelt?" I asked.

My tenth birthday was squeezed in on April 13. In Denmark, decade birthdays are celebrated with special fervor, but my memories of this day's festivities are buried among the more momentous events of the times. Only one detail remains: I received my first telegram. It was from my grandfather, who always knew how to make each member of his family feel special. I pasted it in a little scrapbook with 'Farfar' on the cover where I saved the drawings, pressed flowers, and letters that he sent me from time to time.

A week later, Far joined the other Danish doctors to bring back the concentration camp survivors. Mor and I stayed at home wondering when we would see him again. Mor stopped taking sleeping pills so that she could wake up in the middle of the night if I needed her.

"I never slept as well during the whole war," she told of that time. "It was just too horrible to worry about sleeping."

We heard that Far was back and Mor rushed down to the train station to see him, fresh from the hairdresser and wearing her best spring clothes. She told of the horrors that she saw to all her friends, "I was so glad Ips was back safe, I hurried through the train to find him. The women from the camps were stacked in bunk beds on either side of the aisle, most of them too weak to move. They could barely lift their hands, but clutched at me and touched my dress as I walked down the aisle. Skeletons whispered, blessing me because of the work of my husband, the doctor, their rescuer."

But Far went back to Germany to return again days later, this time with a convoy of buses. Mor and I rushed to the hospital to see him. There the buses were parked, in order to exchange Danish volunteer drivers with those of the Swedish Red Cross, before crossing the Sound to Sweden. As usual I was left outside in the dark to wait and entertain myself. A tall blond Viking stood smoking a cigarette on the top step of a bus doorway. The light spilled out from behind him, onto the grass in ignorant defiance of blackout regulations. I threw my head back to look up at his face when he spoke down to me from the steps. I didn't understand his Swedish, but gratefully accepted a piece of chocolate that he handed me. Chocolate! I had not seen any for a long time. For years afterwards, I thought all Swedes were at least six feet tall, very blonde, and handsome. The prohibition against accepting candy from strange men did not apply; he was not a man, but a hero.

The evening of May 4, we were sitting at the dining table where Far, Mor, and their friend Taj Jerne were playing bridge, and I was drawing. It had been a lovely spring day. Beside Mor on the table were two big balls of light blue yarn. I had outgrown all my sweaters and Mor had unraveled her old wool ski sweater to knit me a new one. The yarn was too thick to make a useful sweater for me, so she had been splitting the four strands into two balls of two-ply yarn. She would unwind about twenty feet of thick wool from its ball and secure the end with a safety pin. Then she went out on the balcony and, dangling the ball over the edge, forced the strands apart while the ball spun madly. Laughing at her own strange antics, and watched by several curious neighbors, she wound up the two new balls of thinner yarn with her usual two-for-one magic.

Just as dusk was falling at 8:30, the time of the nightly news from England, we heard a crescendo of voices from outdoors. Far went out on the balcony and called down, "What's going on?"

"Germany has capitulated," someone yelled back. "We're going to the palace!"

An over-eager radio reporter had prematurely announced the end of the war. Germany was not to agree to a complete surrender for several more days, and Japan's final defeat was three months away. But the delirium of the crowds could not be contained as they flocked with one mind to share the celebration with the ailing King Christian, the national symbol of solidarity.

Taj disappeared out the door to go home. We ran down the stairs, the three of us hand in hand so we wouldn't be separated, and joined the thousands of people streaming across Knippels Bridge toward the palace. There we caught up with Taj, who couldn't move any faster than the rest of us. We passed a young German soldier standing guard on the bridge. Still almost a child, he stood there with his submachine gun, not knowing whether to laugh or cry, run or shoot.

A fellow from the crowd came up and patted him on the back. "Don't worry, now you can go home," he said.

I began to realize that this ordinary child-soldier was no longer the hated enemy, but just a person with a family and a longing for peace like the rest of us. This poignant scene was my first hint that soldiers, even those of the enemy, are as much victims of war as civilians. The devastation in Berlin and London, that we later saw in the newspapers, were far worse than anything we had experienced or could have imagined. Acres of ruins compared to one Jean d'Arc School.

We finally made our way to the Fish Market where I could barely see the statue of Bishop Absolon, the stern warrior staring imperviously down at the tumultuous people of the city he founded. A man had climbed up to the top of the granite pedestal of the statue and was shouting at the crowd.

"Lift me up, I can't see anything," I complained. "What's that man saying?"

"He's speaking for the king, telling us to go home, there's going to be trouble. The war isn't over yet."

"Let's go," said Mor, grabbing me by the hand and Far by the arm. We struggled back across the bridge against the rip-tide of the crowds. All along the way we saw candles in the windows, the hated blackout curtains ripped out, never to be used again.

Peace exploded as the sound of machine-gun fire stilled the cheers.

In all the tumult, Mor had as usual found someone with a story. "Here's a mother and her little girl that can't get home." She told us. "They can sleep in Anne's room and she with us."

The next morning saw a continuation of the most violent part of our war. As we found out later, the German occupation commander of Copenhagen recognized the inevitable and wisely decided to lie low and wait for the official cease-fire; although the gunboats in the harbor were aimed at the city, they remained blessedly silent. The Underground had immediately mobilized and started to round up known collaborators, who rightly feared for their lives and fought back. That was the source of the gunfire we had heard the night before and that continued throughout the day.

Information, one of the Underground newspapers, was miraculously printed and distributed on May 5. "Freedom fighters occupied *Fœdrelandets* building on Kings Broad Street, last night," the lead article proclaimed. It went on to explain that they had feared the workers of that infamous propaganda sheet, *The Fatherland*, would destroy the precious printing presses, so the Underground went to take over the building immediately after the announcement of peace, but found it deserted. The volunteer staffs of *Information* and another paper, *Morgenbladet*, then printed these first editions of freedom, using the appropriated presses. The paper also reported the chaos across the city and the country as various groups of occupation forces and collaborators reacted to the events and uncertainty. It told of the morning arrival of the Danish Brigade from Sweden and the 'invasion' of one hundred advance troops of British General Montgomery, not to mention the ubiquitous foreign press corps. Monty's troops were supposedly mobbed by exuberant girls who tore the soldiers' uniforms to shreds. The paper commented on the ironic contrast between the advance troops of the Allies waving little Danish flags from their flower-bedecked jeeps, and the retreating German soldiers heading for home. The bedraggled and beaten army was so disorganized that soldiers grabbed any form of transportation they could find. Some jammed onto trucks and headed for home, others on bike held on to the side-rails of the trucks for a free ride.

The rector's wife from the Church of Our Savior next door telephoned Mor: "The Underground has a commando station in a basement restaurant on Baadsmands Street. They need a doctor in case there are wounded. Can your husband help?"

Not wanting to be separated, we went down the stairs together, out the door, past the church and my old school. We could hear the sounds of guns in the distance and ran from one doorway to the next, dodging behind the boxes of sand which had protected basement windows against shrapnel. I was terrified. The next day I saw the bullet holes in the wood of some of those boxes.

At the restaurant-bar, people sat around drinking beer and waited for developments. Men and women with the red, blue, and white arm bands of the Underground ran in and out.

I was hysterical with fear. Some heroine! A waitress led me into a little courtyard in the center of the building and persuaded me that I would be safe there. Eventually I calmed down and emerged from my hiding place among the empty wooden crates and other trash, ashamed of my cowardice. For something to do, I helped wait on the beer drinkers. A little boy, son of the proprietors, proudly showed me a real gun. His father had given it to him as reward for keeping the secret of his family's Underground activities. "And he's only eight years old," I marveled.

There never were any wounded, but Far did examine the sore throat of one of the freedom fighters. "He has diphtheria," Far diagnosed, and telephoned for an ambulance from the infectious disease hospital.

The poor man cried. "For years I have waited for this day, and now I have to go to the hospital with a sore throat!" A roving ambulance drove up looking for wounded and spirited the patient away, to the confusion of all when the one that had been ordered showed up.

Rumors flew everywhere. The retired director of the Serum Institute, Thorvald Madsen, told us later that he was at home when Crown Prince Frederick rushed in from the nearby palace. Out of breath but excited by his mad dash, His Highness exclaimed, "A damned lot of barricades one has to jump over these days to get here."

"They say Eisenhower has arrived," said Dr. Madsen.

"Oh sure,— he and my wife just went shopping in town," chuckled the prince.

The next day, Sunday, we stood on top of the rampart by our apartment building because Eisenhower was supposed to be landing at the airport further out on the island. Several hundred people stood there, staring at the sky and waiting for the planes of the 'American invasion.' We willingly manned the old rampart, waiting to welcome the city's liberators.

Eisenhower never materialized, and there was no massing of planes overhead. Little Denmark wasn't important enough. Instead General Montgomery made a triumphal entry by jeep, having landed on the west coast. We waved and cheered the dapper hero as he stood in his car, stiffly saluting the crowds.

"We saw him three times," I bragged. "First on the way into town, then when Mor and I were downtown shopping, he drove by on his way to meet with the king. On our way home, there he was again!"

We stood on the balcony of the famous Hotel d'Angleterre on the King's New Square to watch the Underground's victory parade. Everyone cheered as the different groups with their distinguishing arm bands marched by in disordered clumps. They had no proper uniforms, had never practiced military marching, but arm bands they had. We cheered and waved Danish flags. A truck filled with prisoners passed, the captured collaborators made to stand with their hands on their heads. One man had a minor cut on his head, and the blood was trickling down his face and across his hand. I screamed, much to my parents' embarrassment. It wasn't so much the blood that upset me, but a feeling of betrayal. Those poor people, their arms must be very tired having to stand like that. This isn't peace; it's not right. My heroes in the Underground aren't supposed to hurt anybody.

As usual, Oldemor had the last word. On May 8, 1945, the family gathered around her dining table to celebrate her eighty-eighth birthday. Someone turned on the radio because Churchill was to speak. Everyone rushed into the living room to hear him, leaving Oldemor sitting alone at the table. Over Churchill's dramatic voice, finally announcing the official German surrender, Oldemor was heard to complain, "Why are you all leaving? Don't you want a piece of my birthday cake?"

It was time to return to the important events of everyday life and pick up the pieces of freedom.

Epilogue

A Thousand Bridges

When friends hear my stories they express surprise that I can really remember all these events. At first I too was surprised, not that I can remember my childhood in such detail, but that not everyone else can. My father had almost total recall, not only of what he had experienced, but what he had read and seen and heard. He had an inexhaustible supply of family stories and could quote long poems from memory. His dry wit often contained allusions to literature or to shared events. He laughed with delight when a listener replied in a similar vein. Mother too would regale us with long tales, and when my children were small, entranced them with stories of "when Mommy was a little girl." If she had gone to an afternoon movie, we would hear the whole story in living color that evening. The telling sometimes took longer than the viewing.

I seem to have inherited some of these talents, by nature or by nurture. Those events that I didn't experience directly or didn't clearly remember were told and retold by my parents so that now I cannot distinguish the events themselves from their refreshed memories. It is therefore not strange to me that the war years are still vivid. The smallest incidence can trigger recall; a glimpse becomes a bridge to memory. There are a thousand bridges.

I am flying home at night after a business meeting in Washington and see the lights of Minneapolis twinkling below. I wonder how this city would look from the air with blackout shades at the windows, and street lights and car headlights dimmed. I wake in the early Minnesota winter morning. A fire engine goes by sounding its urgent siren. What an ominous haunting sound. I am only half-awake and sleepily wonder if it is an air raid. Am I supposed to go to the basement? A few stars twinkle at the window through the haze of urban lights. My nose is cold but I am warm under my quilt. The war was like that. As long as we stayed in the warmth of family, we were safe and could ignore the cold outside. The stars of freedom twinkled their reassurance from above.

My mother and I were once discussing my peripatetic adolescence after the war when we sailed back and forth across the Atlantic, lived in several eastern cities in the United States, and I struggled with the alienation of being both a teen-ager and an immigrant.

"Well, at least you had those five stable years when we lived at By The Rampart," said Mor. We smiled at our memories, and the haze of nostalgia completely obscured the fact that those 'good old days' were in the midst of the terror of a world war.

During one of my periodic trips to Copenhagen, I visit the apartment buildings by the rampart. It is the same but also different. The pond where we skated and had snowball fights has been made smaller to make way for an enlarged parking lot. The cement on the balconies is stained, giving the complex a worn and seedy look. It was prettier when new, and when only bikes were parked along the side and children played on the drive.

Four years after the war, we moved into another new red brick apartment building with balconies, but this time along the Charles River in Cambridge, Massachusetts. It was the first post-war apartment building in town. We watched its construction all that long hot summer when we went down to the river to escape the heat in our third-floor Boston apartment. Across the river the massive buildings of MIT were lit by spot lights as dusk fell and the new apartment building slowly grew next door. The architects had studied Scandinavian apartment designs. It looked comfortably like By The Rampart, and Mor decided it would be our new home.

We take my little son to the palace to see the changing of Queen Margrethe's guards. She is the granddaughter of the revered Christian X whose statue stands at the entrance as a memorial to his leadership during the war. The taller-than-life soldier now perpetually rides his horse and smiles paternally down at his people. The new generation of tall guards in their red uniforms and tall, black, beaver hats march every morning from their billets by Rosenborg, Cinderella's castle, across town to the palace. Policemen walk alongside for crowd control. Are these small, ordinary men in blue there to protect those magnificent giants? I recall the German soldiers in green, goose-stepping through town. The same image but so different; the watchers on the sidewalk are smiling, and the only shooting is with cameras.

My husband and I visit Denmark every few years, not just Copenhagen but also other parts of the country. The ferries constantly crisscross *Store Belt*—The Big Belt, the channel of water between the two largest islands of Zealand and Fyn. The plans for building a bridge are perennial; it is now under construction, but not quite believed in by anyone. As the train smoothly drives onto the ferry, never disturbing my sleeping husband, I think of that Christmas crossing in 1944, the long lines walking onto the ferry, the inspections, the delays. The feelings of that long ago trip come back every time I pass through US Customs, with the crowds and vague air of suspicion that even I, this graying matron, may be trying to get away with something.

These days, more than fifty years after the war, I am the grandparent who is visited for holidays. Now it is the 'grandparent' part that is the great adventure. The gathering in Minneapolis of grandchildren, daughters, son, and son-in-law from distant states is always a pleasure, and this newer part of the family has evolved its own Christmas rituals and "do-you-remember-when" stories. But the trips themselves, in this day of jet travel, are taken for granted, winter storms the only inconvenience. I look back in some awe at the willingness of those know-better adults to undertake what was in 1944 a difficult trip for the sake of a week of organized chaos.

Thus the war left small, strange scars. Although we never had the severe hardships of the front lines and other places in Europe, the aftereffects of the oppressive atmosphere, fears, hassles, shortages, and having-to-cope became a permanent part of us—to crop up at unexpected times. "Think of the starving Norwegians" was supposed to encourage me to finish my dinner, but only tempted me to be sassy and suggest shipping the leftovers to where they would be more appreciated. It was no more meaningful than "the poor Belgians" of the previous war had been for my parents. What a strange threat, unlikely to increase anyone's appetite. Yet throwing away uneaten food still bothers me—or wasting paper, or electricity.

I remember Mor's fury when we left on our second trip to the U.S.A. Swedish ship officers had thoughtlessly but innocently put stickers bearing yellow stars on our suitcases to separate the luggage of passengers embarking at Copenhagen from those already on board. "How can you use yellow stars," she raged. "What if some of the passengers are Jewish? How do you suppose they feel!"

Or, when Mor yelled at an usher in an American movie theater kept us behind a rope until the audience from an earlier show had left, "Stop acting like a Nazi, ordering me around and telling me where I can go!" Was she remembering being herded at that ferry?

Or exasperated Far, when he couldn't convince a Boston-Italian barber that he liked his hair longer in the back: "You'll make me look like a Nazi soldier!"

I recently saw a TV interview with Mr. Koppel, the famous and honored pianist-composer, who had been our Jewish neighbor, now old and venerable. He spoke of his family, including his eldest daughter, now a singer, with whom I shared my beloved piano teacher so long ago. I felt very strange seeing him. I remembered Far's piano lessons with him. Most of all, his family's hurried escape to Sweden was linked in my mind with Cousin Clara's terrible experiences.

The rescue of the Danish Jews stands as a beacon in the history of that troubled time. It also meant that after the war Denmark could stand tall with the other nations that resisted tyranny. A vague and suppressed feeling that Denmark had been cooperating and even collaborating with evil was replaced by a pride that, after all, Moral Right had prevailed. Yet that pride was modest; one does not brag about doing good.

When I was old enough to read about and understand this remarkable story, I too was proud. I absorbed it as a model of how weak individuals can win against those with power by stubbornly acting together. Although I was too young to take an active part, I felt I could take some credit just for being there and passively resisting wrong.

I still have many treasures from those days. I look at my old drawings in the sketchbooks on which Ulla and I spent so many happy hours and that Mor faithfully saved. They are full of flowers, trees, primitive stick figures, friends, make-believe, and daily happenings. There is no hint of anything to do with the war, or school for that matter, just Danish flags, half-told stories, and misspellings. Next to them on my bookcase is the photo album. It too is devoid of war. The images of the little girl, her friends and family; the scenes from school, the play yard, and the country could be from anyone's ordinary childhood.

From my maternal grandmother, whom I never met, I have only a few precious things. Two pictures of her survive and hang on my wall: my grandmother as a little girl with a big lace collar and as a young woman with two of her sons and Mor as children. I also have a worn silver-plate nail cleaner and a tiny sterling coffee spoon. But I do have the stories Mor told of her childhood: of standing by her parents' bed to get a coin for scout dues, and of her mother buying the first tomatoes. I see Mor gesturing to show how her mother lifted the large veil on her fashionable hat when she bent down to kiss her little daughter good-bye on the way to a party.

The heritage from Far's side of the family is more abundant. Oldemor's pearls are in my jewelry box, waiting to be restrung. Her picture is at her namesake granddaughter's house, my Aunt Christel; but her father, the admiral, and her son, my grandfather, smile at me from among the pictures of my American family hanging on the wall over my computer. We are seven generations.

Most of Aunt Agathe's dinner plates, soup plates, and multitude of serving dishes are at Aunt Christel's house, together with the picture of Oldemor, but I have the magnificent tureen. I use it with great ceremony to serve chicken soup. Aunt Agathe's sampler has been framed and hangs in my study. It reminds me to be grateful that, although I do needlework with great pleasure and was taught other 'accomplishments' thought suitable for a young lady a hundred years ago, I was allowed far more education and choice of how to live, than these two sisters.

The picture album has many photos of the house at Esrum. Our final stay there was after we had moved to America. Mor, my friend Carol, and I spent two weeks at the house after the two of us were graduated from high school. Ulla came too for a happy-sad visit. Mor took a snapshot of the three of us standing under the branches of the Japanese cherry tree, the full branches spreading over our heads. We made a compatible threesome, the spoken language barrier only slight; our imaginations and body language forged instant bonds. Ulla still had the same thin pale face, blond hair, and slightly protruding blue eyes. I was surprised that we were all the same height; she used to be at least a head taller than I.

Carol later shared a description of Ulla from her journal of those days: "Her neck was beautiful and her thin lips had a little wrinkle in each corner when she smiled. She was slender in her pants and every time she walked, a tendon or bone would ripple under the skin."

A few years later, Mor and Far told me they had sold the house to the couple that had been renting it for several years. It needed repairs, and the renters wanted to buy it so they could fix it up. My heart wept.

More recently, we were on our way to lunch by the Sound north of Copenhagen. We drove up the little dirt road and stopped by the house. No one was home, but we peeked through the windows and saw the indoor plumbing and a telephone. In back, a manicured lawn edged with well-pruned trees sloped down to the lake. There were new vacation houses on the old fields next door. The lake was still beautiful, but the land was too civilized. Everything was much smaller than I remembered.

The red lamp was no longer there, but I saw its spirit hanging from a rafter, an umbrella protecting our sanctuary. Truly it was a magic Aladdin lamp: Mor polished it and we got her wish, our dream house.

I wish I could say that Mor had a long and happy life, but her difficult childhood, the stresses of the war, and the challenge of making a new life in the USA finally caught up with her. When I left for college and no longer wanted her constant attention to my life, she lost the primary purpose in hers. She had carefully prepared me to stand on my own feet and make my own decisions, but forgot to prepare herself for my independence. At about the same age that her mother had given up and committed suicide, it was as if Mor lost her model of how to live. Although she survived another twenty years, the spark was gone. She started to drink, not large amounts, but just enough so that the combination with her continuing dependence on sleeping pills spelled disaster for her mind and body. Most of the time she merely existed in a fog of chemically induced escape. Finally one kidney failed and had to be removed, her liver was damaged, and she suffered a bout with ileitis from which she never recovered. She slipped into a coma. As I held her hand, I remembered the summer I was ill and couldn't stand in church, and Mor's comforting hand on mine.

That simple gesture of love has stayed with me, an expression of her constant care.

My friend Carol told me that during one late-night conversation, Mor exclaimed, "Didn't you always want to do something wonderful?" When I look at my three grown children, I think she has. They are continual reminders of Mor. When they were little and we went places, I remembered her spirit of adventure; when we cooked or sewed together I saw her hands instead of mine. The family photographs smile down at me as I type these lines. My young mother's face, as I saw her returning from southern Europe the summer before the war, is repeated in each family grouping over years of Christmas pictures. I recognize our dimpled smiles and prominent chins. Mor's portrait with the marcelled hair and white ruffled collar on her long swan neck, is mirrored in that of her granddaughter, Elizabeth, the bride with the lace trim around the broad shoulders and the graceful dancer's neck. My throat still catches when I am surprised by a familiar expression on Elizabeth's face.

The adult Elizabeth's voice is faint in the next room as she talks on the telephone to a friend or perhaps a patient. Her soprano voice is higher than Mor's was when she chatted to strangers on the bus or wrangled food from a shopkeeper, but Elizabeth's talent for listening to people came directly from her grandmother, skipping the proverbial generation and becoming full-blown in the clinical psychologist. Jonathan does have her deep voice, as well as the chin and the dimples, but the rebellious hair and infectious laugh are indubitably Far's. Alison may have inherited her father's build, but the chin, strong character, and independent spirit came from Mor.

I had wonderful intellectual mentors in both Far and Farfar. Far was a continuing guide, but Farfar had taught him and was a strong influence in my childhood and adolescence. A print of the white-coated scientist-as-young-man hangs in my office. A microscope is in front of him on the table surrounded by mysterious bottles with Latin inscriptions. An assistant hovers in the back-ground. The picture is from an illustration in an old textbook on laboratory methods. My cousin Jens, the clinical biochemist, discovered it and gave me a copy. Is that the same microscope Farfar later used for his amateur naturalist studies? The one he carefully took out of its wooden case to show me how he had drawn million-year-old flies trapped in amber?

With pride I place daughter Elizabeth's doctoral thesis next to mine on the bookcase. Four generations of books stand tall together: Farfar's, Far's, mine, and now Elizabeth's. Perhaps there will be more.

I look at the old newspaper clippings from Far's thesis defense that Mor kept in a scrapbook and remember my first formal party afterward. By contrast, the defense of my thesis was much less impressive. I merely mailed the manuscript to Harvard after it had been duly approved by my advisor and reader. It was then placed 'on the table' in the departmental office for the faculty to see, and a week later I was notified that I had passed. *The Boston Globe* paid no attention.

A colleague at the University of Minnesota told me that during the 1950's there was a patient at University Hospital with an illness that no one had been able to diagnose. An old, experienced nurse was walking through the corridor. "I smell diphtheria," she said, sniffing audibly, and solved the mystery. The attending doctors had never seen a case. I mentioned the diphtheria epidemic in Denmark and remembered Far's tales of inoculating long lines of patients, and my first experience helping him tally data.

Now it is hard to realize the constant fear of infectious diseases which was an undercurrent during my childhood and before that time. Diphtheria and small pox were preventable with vaccines and I, the daughter of an expert, was always well-inoculated. The usual childhood diseases—measles, chicken pox, German measles, and mumps—were taken for granted as something one needed to get out of the way as quickly as possible. But tuberculosis, scarlet fever and poliomyelitis invoked terror because they were thought to be highly contagious, the morbidity and mortality were devastating, and they were largely untreatable except with bedrest. Mor's brother had tuberculosis and died young; Far had caught a mild case as an intern, but recovered entirely and never relapsed. Mor's fear that I would catch it became a snobbish obsession to keeping me away from 'poor' children. She was not happy when I sometimes played with the children who lived on the slum street in back of our apartment complex, but at least we were outside in the fresh air.

My illness during the spring and summer of 1944 was, of course, not caused by an infection, but was certainly a dramatic event. I learned many lessons about the importance of family and emotional support, but was also engaged by the science discussed around me. I recently decided to look for the article by the Boston doctor which led Dr. Chievitz to the proper treatment. I guessed that the crucial article must have appeared in the *New England Journal of Medicine* and searched the indexes of old volumes, starting with 1944 and going backwards. I looked for 'eosinophilic' and for 'granuloma' without success. Getting discouraged, my eyes strayed from the title index of one 1942 volume to the 'Gs' of the author index and suddenly I saw "Dr. Green." "That's him!" I exclaimed. This was a minor miracle, considering my notorious inability to recall even the most familiar of names.

There it was, one of the traditional *New England Journal of Medicine* 'case histories' from the Massachusetts General Hospital, in the form of a vivid dialogue between physicians. The patient's history was very different from mine; she was seventeen and had a large lesion on her skull—actually a hole causing partial paralysis of the face. Dr. Green carefully described his differential diagnosis, choosing between multiple myeloma, osteomylitis, and Hand-Schüller-Christian syndrome, all frightening-sounding alternatives. He also said that he felt this latter was "associated with lesions of the skull" and was an earlier or less virulent form of fatal Letterer-Siwe disease. He felt that both were variants of 'eosinophilic granuloma of the bone.' He and a Dr. Farber had published an article a few months earlier describing ten such cases in children of various ages, some with single lesions in the pelvis—just like me. They had used small doses of radiation treatment with complete cures and no aftereffects—just like me.

I felt strange standing there holding the dusty volume, as if I were accidentally eaves-dropping on the echoes of a conversation. The article was dated November 26, 1942, well after the entry of the USA into the war. By what devious route had that journal migrated across international borders and war fronts to be read at a crucial time by Danish doctors in May of 1944? I found the other article too, in the *Journal of Bone and Joint Surgery* from July of the same year. The co-author was Sidney Farber. A famous children's cancer institute by the Harvard Medical School now bears his name.

Shortly before Far died, I called him at the nursing home. I told him that I had had a picture framed. His wife is an artist, a printmaker, and she had given it to me a few months earlier. I remarked on her talent.

"I think you have a lot of talent too," he said.

"I had a good teacher," I answered.

Far paused to catch his failing breath, but finally said, sounding puzzled, "Yes, your Grandfather was a fine painter and taught you a lot."

"I meant you," I explained.

"But I can't paint," he protested.

"I wasn't talking about painting."

I'm glad I said that. I never talked to Far again or had a chance to wish him a happy birthday. He died the day before he would have been eighty-three.

At his funeral, I think of all the times he carried me the summer of my illness and how he suffered from a bad back forever after. The family is walking from the church to the cemetery where Far is to be buried next to his father, stepmother, and younger brother. His four sisters are sitting on a bench at the entrance waiting for us. I carry the urn with his ashes and walk down the road, remembering. My arms cradle him as his used to hold me. He is much lighter than I was that summer.

Departing for the United States, March 1946.

About the Author

Anne Ipsen was born in Denmark where she lived during the Second World War and German occupation. After the war, she and her parents traveled in the United States and finally settled in Boston, where she graduated from Radcliffe and eventually received her doctorate from Harvard University. In 1970 Anne, her husband, and their three children moved to Minneapolis. She is now a professor at the University of Minnesota and the author of numerous papers in professional journals. This memoir is her first literary publication.